art words

ISBN 978 0 9547552 4 9

British Library Cataloguing-in-Publication Data
A catalogue record for this book is available
from The British Library

By the same author:
Modern Africa (with R B Sutcliffe)
Africa from Early Times
Nineteenth Century Africa
Twentieth Century Africa
Industrial Organisations and Health
(with F Baker and A Sheldon)
Retirement (with A Sheldon and C Ryser)
The Dictionary of Scottish Art and Architecture
To Catch the Moon from the Bottom of the Sea

Typeset in 8/10pt Georgia
Printed in China through Colorcraft Ltd, Hong Kong

Published by Glengarden Press
Ballater, Aberdeenshire AB35 5UB
www.glengardenpress.com
Tel: 013397 55429

art words

The Handbook of Art & Art Related Terms

Peter McEwan

Glengarden Press

INTRODUCTION

It is hoped that this little book will help all who are interested in art and other fine objects but who may not always be aware of the artistic lexicon.

To keep within the bounds of the portable, this is an ABC not a dictionary. Excluded are common names and words of everyday use such as auctioneer, insurance. This means that while 'Schools of Art' have one generic entry, it would have been impracticable within the space available to list individual schools, the few exceptions being included because of their particular influence or popularity.

Extremely esoteric or coined terms unlikely to be encountered also do not appear, similarly there is no mention of the large variety of colours now available, the details of which are only likely to interest practitioners and which can be found in the catalogue of any good colourman.

The worlds of ceramics, furniture, heraldry and silver have all been touched upon, as well as classical architecture which provides so many of the terms used in picture framing and, to a lesser degree, in furniture design.

Some words are best described visually. These have been illustrated. I am enormously grateful to my friend the architect and artist Alison Ewan who has provided all the drawings.

Entries closely related to other entries appear in the text in bold except where their names closely coincide with each other in which case they are shown in small capitals e.g. under the entry **bargeboards**, BARGECOURSE appears in small capitals, since it has no entry of its own, whereas **gableboards** is in bold because it also has its own entry.

References in foreign languages e.g. botanical names, are shown in *italics*. Words of foreign origin that have passed into accepted English (e.g. avant garde) are not italicised. This is sometimes arbitrary and the arbiter has been the Oxford English Dictionary.

An enormous amount of work has been done in design and proofing, quite disproportionate to the size of the book, by Chic Harper, my son Rhod, and Moira McDougall, to all of whom I extend my most sincere gratitude.

For any errors, which I trust are few, I am alone responsible. But do please let me know of omissions which you would like to have seen included.

Peter McEwan

abacus

In architecture, and also in **Sansovino** and **tabernacle** frames, an abacus is a square slab on top of a **capital**, supporting the **architrave**. The shape of an abacus has varied down the ages, thick and square in the **Doric**, thinner and ornamented in the **Ionic**, with truncated corners and concave sides in the **Corinthian**. A rounded form has become more popular in modern times. Not to be confused with an ABACULUS, a small tile used in making mosaics.

abacus

abatement(s)

In heraldry, a mark of disgrace. The only abatements still in common use are marks of illegitimacy.

abbreviations

The following are the most common abbreviations for art establishments and artists' affiliations.

AAS	Aberdeen Artists Society
ARA	Associate Royal Academy
ARE	Associate Royal Academy of Painters and Etchers
ARHA	Associate Royal Hibernian Academy
ARIAS	Associate Royal Incorporation of Architects in Scotland
ARIBA	Associate Royal Institute of British Architects
ARMS	Associate Royal Society of Miniature Painters
ARPE	Associate Royal Society of Painters-Etchers
ARSA	Associate Royal Scottish Academy
ARWS	Associate Royal Society of Painters in Watercolours
ASL	Associate, Society of Limners
BM	British Museum
FAS	Fellow Antiquarian Society
FBA	Fellow British Academy
FRIAS	Fellow Royal Incorporation of Architects in Scotland
FRIBA	Fellow Royal Institute of British Architects

A

FRS Fellow Royal Society
FRSA Fellow Royal Society of Arts
FRSE Fellow Royal Society of Edinburgh
FRSSA Fellow Royal Scottish Society
FRSA Fellow Royal Society of Antiquaries
FSA Fellow Royal Society of Artists (pre-1971)
GI/RGI (Royal) Glasgow Institute of the Fine Arts
HRSA Hon Member Royal Scottish Academy
NEAC New English Art Club
NG National Gallery
NLS National Library of Scotland
NPG National Portrait Gallery
NWS New Watercolour Society
OWS Old Water Colours Society or Society of Painters in Watercolours, later Royal Society of Painters in Watercolours
PRA President Royal Academy
PPRA Past President Royal Academy
PRCA President Royal Cambrian Academy
PRHA President Royal Hibernian Academy
PRI President Royal Institute of Painters in Watercolours
PRMS President Royal Miniature Society
PRSA President Royal Scottish Academy
PPRSA Past President, Royal Scottish Academy
RA Royal Academy/Royal Academician
RBA Royal Society of British Artists (Suffolk Street)
RCA Member Royal Cambrian Academy
RCanA Royal Canadian Academy
RE Fellow Royal Society of Painters and Etchers
RHA Royal Hibernian Academy/Royal Hibernian Academician
RHCA Hon. Member Royal Cambrian Academy
RI Royal Institute of Painters in Watercolours
RIBA Royal Institute of British Architects
RMS Royal Society of Miniature Painters, Sculptors and Engravers
ROI Royal Institute of Oil Painters
RSA Royal Scottish Academy/Royal Scottish Academician. *Also*, Royal Society of Arts.
RSW Royal Scottish Society of Painters in Watercolours
RWA Royal West of England Academy
RWS Royal Society of Watercolour Painters
SA Society of Artists (1765)
SBA Society of British Artists (Royal Society of British Artists)
SM Society of Miniaturists (Limners)
SNGMA Scottish National Gallery of Modern Art
SNPG Scottish National Portrait Gallery
SS Suffolk Street (see RBA)
SSA Scottish Society of Artists
SSWA Scottish Society of Women Artists
V&A Victoria & Albert Museum
VPRI Vice-President Royal Institute of Painters in Water Colours
VPRMS Vice-President Royal Society of Miniature Painters, Sculptors and Engravers
WIAC Women's International Art Club

See also **del**, **fl**, **fecit**, **pinxit**.

abstract art
Art which does not seek to represent recognisable reality, preferring to concentrate on colour, form and shape. A distinction is sometimes made between loosely painted images, the romantic, and the hard-edged geometric type, the classical. Abstract art originated shortly before the first world war, subsequently spawning many movements and styles, as, for example, **Cubism, Dadaism, Futurism**.

Abstract Expressionism
An art movement centred on New York in the mid 20th century. An offshoot of **Surrealism**, its exponents focussed on creative spontaneity.

Abstract-Création movement
A diverse association of artists, formed in Paris in 1931, who joined forces in seeking to counter the growing influence of **Surrealism**.

academic art
The kinds of classical paintings and sculptures produced by students trained at the pre-war academic establishments of the west. Most specifically, it refers to the characteristic products of the 19th century French Academy.

academy
Originally an academy referred to the open space on the edge of Athens where Plato taught, christened after Academus. The term came to describe any teaching institution. Thus, in art, most western countries and major regions have their art-related academies, in France, for example, there is the Académie Française, in London, the Royal Academy.

acanthus
A stylised version of the acanthus stem and leaf, often used in the decoration of **Corinthian** columns. A pattern also used as an ornament for frames. Derived from the acanthus design used in Roman architecture, based upon plants of the order *Acanthaceæ*.

acanthus

acanthus-and-tongue
An ornamental design of acanthus leaves alternating with plain **tongues**. Often applied to the **sight edge** of **Carlo Maratta** frames, sometimes with a shell instead of a tongue.

accosted
An heraldic term meaning placed side by side. For animals the French word *accosté* is used; when referring to shields the term is *accolé*.

achromatic
Work executed without colour, using black, white and/or greys.

A

acid tint
The production of a delicate grain in an **aquatint** obtained by leaving powdered sulphur on the surface of the plate which can then be lightly feathered to produce a **textile grain**. *Vide* **sulphur tint**.

acroterium
In classical times, a small pedestal to support a statue. Also refers to the ornament itself. Also known as an ACROTER or ACROTERION.

acrylic
A painting medium made from acrylic acid, in a form commonly extracted from synthetic compounds. The effect is slightly harsher than traditional **watercolour** but does not fade.

action painting
An American description ascribed to the critic Harold Rosenberg, which gave importance to the random physical application of paint, regardless of the effects. The foremost adherent was the American painter Jackson Pollock (1912-1956). Pollock would place a canvas on the floor and proceed to cover it with paint, sometimes mixing it with sand or broken glass.

Adam style
A style of architecture and related furniture stemming from the work of the Edinburgh architect and interior designer Robert Adam (1728-1792), in association with his brother James (1730-1794). They introduced a lighter more decorative approach, exemplified by Register House in Edinburgh and Syon House, Middlesex.

ad(d)orsed
Heraldic term meaning back to back.

adularia
Vide **feldspar**.

ad vivum
When appearing beneath a portrait print it indicates that the print was taken from life rather than from a painting.

adytum
The innermost recess of an ancient temple, into which only the specially privileged were permitted to enter. The term has come to describe anything inaccessible.

aedicule
A small Roman chapel; a recess for an altar or statue.

Aesthetic Movement
An English artistic movement of the 1880s dedicated to the idea of beauty and hence 'art for art's sake', regardless of morality, which exerted considerable influence on important formal elements in art. Its best known proponents were Aubrey Beardsley (1872-1898), Sir Henry Beerbohm (1872-1956) and, in literature, Oscar Wilde (1854-1900).

aesthetics
The study and philosophy of **beauty**. More loosely, it refers to principles of good taste and appreciation of beauty according to the standards of the age.

agate
The least valuable of precious stones. A kind of **quartz**, unique in having bands or layers of colour blended together. When polished it is used for making **burnishers**, mortars, pestles and boxes in the decorative arts. There is a secondary meaning in the printing trade where an agate is a print size of about 160 lines per foot, commonly used in newspapers.

agora
In ancient Greece an agora was political and general public discussion. By extension, it became the name for the chief meeting place in a town.

agraffe
An ornate fastener used on both armour and normal dress, often richly decorated with jewels or enamels.

aiguilettes
The metal ties of the ribbons used to fasten portions of dress during the 16th and 17th centuries. Aiguilettes, or AIGLETTES, were often seen, for example, in the portraits of Hans Holbein (1497-1543). Not to be confused with **ailettes**.

ailettes
Small square-shaped wings attached to the shoulders of knights in armour, sometimes carrying heraldic bearings.

aisle
The wing of a building. An open passage way in a church parallel to the **nave** from which it is usually divided by columns.

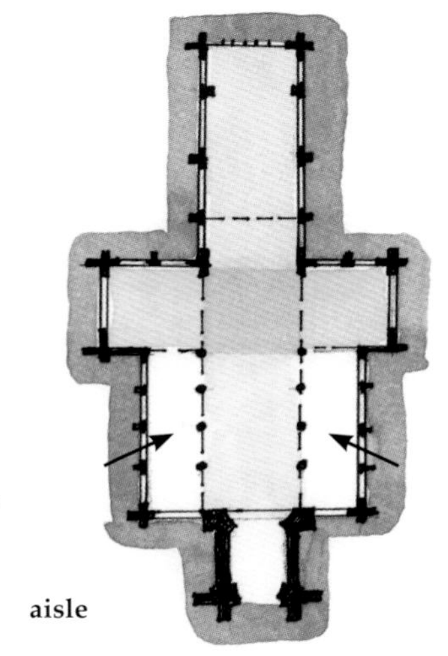

aisle

Nowadays applied to the passage way in any place of public assembly.

alabaster
Vide **gypsum**.

albarello
An upright earthenware container for keeping drugs, common in the 15th century. The usual shape is cylindrical with a concave central stem. The term is derived from the Italian word for a tree trunk.

albumen print
Albumen is a chemical extracted from egg white, sometimes used in photographic printing processes when albumen is used in the emulsion.

alfresco
In the open air; same as ***en plein air***.

A

alhambra

alhambra
Type of frame common in the mid 19th century, characterised by a wide **hollow** decorated with **Moresque** or similar intricate small-scale ornament, with a prominent rounded top edge on which corner motifs may be placed. It later became used to describe a richly decorated frame of convex or **ogee** profile and ornamental **top edge**. The term is derived from the arabic word for a red castle, specifically an architecturally outstanding Moorish castle, near Granada, built 1248-1354.

alla prima
A method of painting whereby paint is applied without any under-painting. From the Italian for 'at once'. Finished work of this kind is called an *ABBOZZO*.

allegory
The figurative, symbolic representation of meaning in a painting or sculpture.

alloy
An artificial mixture of two or more metals.

altarpiece
A decorative screen placed behind an altar, often a painting. *Vide* **reredos**.

alum
An umbrella term for a class of soluble sulphates using aluminium, iron and some sulphates. Its principal use in the arts is as a **mordant** in the manufacture of dyes.

amateur
When used to describe an artist the term has come to have two meanings. The etymologically correct meaning describes someone who does not depend upon the activity for commercial gain. The pejorative use denotes an inferior practitioner.

amboyna
A distinctive dark coloured wood used in furniture making. From the south east Asian tree *Pterocarpus indicus*.

American Arts & Crafts Movement
Vide **Arts & Crafts Movement**.

amethyst
A precious stone of a violet or purple colour, due to peroxide of iron. In heraldry it refers to the tincture *purpura(y)*.

amorino(i)
Cupid(s) – a motif common in Roman decorative art and popular toward the end of the 17th century and again toward 1750. Sometimes loosely applied to the appearance of children in art.

amphora
An early drinking vessel with two handles and a narrow neck.

amulet
An ornament or small piece of jewellery superstitiously worn as a charm against accidents, evil and witchcraft. Occasionally figures in early paintings. Amulets have been found in the **catacombs**, many of them inscribed with the word *ichthys* (fish) representing the initials of the Greek words for Jesus Christ. An amulet is different to a **TALISMAN** which is intended to ensure a desired result for the wearer.

Analytical art
Vide **Futurism**.

Analytical Cubism
Vide **Cubism**.

anastatic printing
A process for making facsimiles of prints, dependent on the incompatibility of ink and water. A weak solution of phosphoric acid in gum and water is used to moisten the print which is then pressed on to a zinc sheet. The reverse impression on the zinc sheet is then wetted. An inked roller is passed across the plate leaving ink only on the impressed lines. The impression thus pulled from the inked plate provides an exact facsimile.

Anatolian carpets
Vide **Oriental carpets**.

angiport
A narrow passage or port in the wall of a fortified building either to fire from or as an easily protected entrance.

aniline
A colourless, oily liquid used in the manufacture of dyes. The first harsh colours with aniline were used in early **chromolithography** in the mid 1850s. Charles Joseph Hullmandel (1789-1850) was largely responsible for the development of finer textures and tones of aniline coloured inks.

anta
Refers to either (a) a support for a wall such as a buttress, or (b) a kind of pilaster or SPERONE. When the support is in the form of more than one anta the components are called ANTAE.

antefix
A decoration of stylised foliage placed above a **pediment**. Small upright tiles on a roof are called ANTEFIXAE.

antependium
Borrowed from church architecture where it refers to a fabric hanging in front of an altar. In **tabernacle** frames it refers to decoration applied to the lower portion, often in the form of a **volute** or **helix**.

anthemion
A floral ornament of alternating palmettes and honeysuckle linked by **acanthus** and small spiral **volutes**.

anthemion

antimacassar
A decorative loose lining on the arms and backs of chairs to guard against stain from macassar hair oil.

antimony
A brittle white metal used in the making of many alloys including the manufacture of **pewter**.

antipagment
Vide **architrave**.

Antipodeans
A short lived group of seven 20th century Australian artists who upheld the values of figurative art in the face of the advance of abstract art and its American influence.

antiquarian
Relating to the study of antiquities. A subsidiary meaning describes paper measuring 53 x 31 or 52 x 29 inches.

antique
An object of considerable age, beyond the modern, specifically of ancient times. One hundred years is sometimes used as the criterion but this is arbitrary. In bookbinding it is used misleadingly to describe modern binding executed in the style of an earlier period. The term also has a specific use in papermaking, denoting a particular kind of rough, unrolled paper.

Aphrodite
Greek goddess of **beauty** and love.

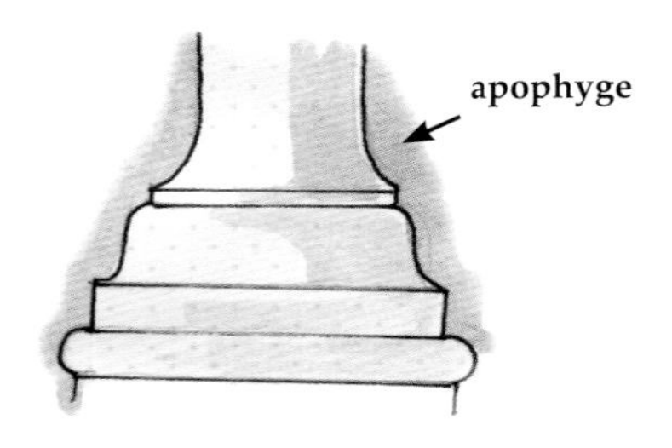

apophyge
Part of an architectural column of concave shape where the shaft rises from the base. Also known as the **scape** or SPRING of the column.

Apostles
In early Christian art the apostles were represented as sheep. Later they appeared as individual men, often with attributes showing the instrument(s) of their martyrdom. Thus St Peter is shown with a key, or fish; St Paul with a sword; St John a cup; St Andrew a saltire; St James the Greater, a sword or pilgrim's staff; St Philip a pastoral staff; St James the Lesser a club; St Bartholomew a knife or processional cross; St Simon a saw; St Jude a lance; St Thomas a builder's rule or a lance; St Matthias an axe or a sword.

appelotype
A seldom used type of **mezzotint** developed by Ackermann for the purpose of reproducing sketchy brush strokes.

appliqué
Ornamental work in which material, usually of fabric or wood, is cut out and attached to the main item.

apse
A semi-circular or polygonal recess in a church beyond the **choir**, usually towards the eastern end.

aqua fortis
Nitric acid. Used by etchers to facilitate corrosion of the metal plate. Thus an AQUAFORTIST is an etcher.

aquæmanale
A small water container for washing hands, often of grotesque shape.

aquatint
A print made to look like a watercolour by using a copper plate sprinkled with a mastic powder or similar substance. This assumes a granular form preventing the nitric acid from acting on the copper where the particles adhere. Thus the copper is only partially corroded with a result resembling a wash of **India ink**. It grew out of fashion in the 19th century but has recently enjoyed a revival.

arabesque
Any design or ornament of intertwined animals, birds, leaves or scrolls. Usually fanciful, varying according to their place of origin. Thus Islamic art forbids animal forms whereas Western art, influenced by Raphael, considered all members of the animal kingdom for inclusion.

architectonic
Pertaining to architecture.

architrave
A type of picture frame identified in the 18th century as a **Kent frame**. Derived from the architectural term for the moulded frame around a window or doorway, or the exterior of an arch. Also known as an **archivolt** or **antipagment**.

archivolt
In picture frames, an arched **architrave**.

arcuate
Bow-shaped; curvilinear.

armature
In sculpture, an armature is the supporting framework, generally of metal and occasionally of wood, around which is moulded the sculpture.

arris
A sharp edge formed by the meeting of two flat or curved surfaces. In picture framing it refers to the sharp edge of the **moulding**.

art
No word in the English language is prone to greater debate or more varied interpretation. A dictionary definition 'human creative skill or its application', begs the question: what is 'creative', and how does it differ from 'craft' which is defined as 'skill, especially in the practical arts'? The Russian philosopher Kralic identified five arts corresponding to our five senses: the art of the sense of taste, the art of the sense of smell, the art of the sense of touch, the art of the sense of hearing, and the art of the sense of sight.

In more modern times Ruskin demanded beauty as an intrinsic, necessary component of any work of 'art'. The critic Clive Bell argued that what he called 'significant form' is an essential quality. In his great essay *What is Art?* Tolstoy concluded 'to evoke in oneself a feeling one has once experienced and having evoked it in oneself then by means of movements, lines, colours, sounds, or forms expressed in words, so to transmit that feeling that others experience the same feeling – this is the activity of art. Art is a human activity consisting in this, that one man consciously by means of external signs, hands on to others a feeling that he has lived through, and that others are infected by these feelings and also experience them'. It is the quality of the feeling, Tolstoy argues, that makes the difference between 'good' and 'bad' art. In the last analysis an individual must decide for him/herself what are the essential components before something can be thought of as 'art', a decision which although subjectively made should be founded as far as possible on objective grounds, otherwise there is nihilism.
A modern fallacy is to presume that the terms 'artist' and 'painter' are synonymous. There is, of course, the quite different use of the term 'art', when, for example, we speak of the art of mixing cocktails or the art of doing crossword puzzles, when what is meant is 'technique'. These disparate meanings, creative art and technique, sometimes appear to merge as when we speak of the art of perspective or the art of photography. Whether the merger is genuine depends on how one defines art.

When used to describe paper, 'art' refers to the glossy variety. When describing covering material, (eg ART VELLUM) 'art' is an abbreviation for 'artificial'.

Art Deco

An international movement in the decorative arts, at its height between 1922 and 1939. Characterised by geometric shapes, vivid colours and clearcut edges. Appearances were most suited to opulent architecture, domestic decoration and home appliances; the most typical materials used were bronze, chrome, glass and stone. The movement in the United States continued until the outbreak of the Second Great War. The term originated as the abbreviated form of the *Exposition Internationale des Arts Decoratifs et Industriels*, held in Paris in 1925.

art form

Any medium of artistic expression.

Art Nouveau

A style of decorative art in the 1890s and early 1900s characterised by complex curvilinear designs and motifs based on natural, asymmetrical forms. Leading exponents included Hector Guimard (1867-1942), Charles Rennie Mackintosh (1868-1928), Aubrey Beardsley (1872-1898), Emile Gallé (1846-1904), and the Czech painter and poster designer Alphonse Mucha (1860-1939). Although comparatively short-lived, being a reaction to the academic art of the 19th century, it helped to establish the **De Stijl** group in Holland and the **Bauhaus** movement in Germany. The movement was known in Germany as ***Jugendstil*** ('youth style').

art schools

The term has two quite separate meanings. It can refer to the followers of a particular leader, group or period, with specific identifiable traits e.g. the School of Rembrandt, the Newlyn School. It can also refer to a place of artistic instruction, most commonly known as the '... School of Art'. Occasionally these distinct meanings merge, as when the latter generates a recognisable idiosyncratic style among its pupils, as, for example, the **Glasgow School** and the Glasgow School of Art.

Arte Povera

An Italian art movement of the mid 20th century. The common factor was a desire to explore new concepts and new processes. Italian precursor to **conceptual art**.

artisan

A skilled craftsman or manual worker. ARTISAN MANNERISM is an architectural term describing 17th century buildings with deficient or inexact features of the **Classical** model.

artist

A person who engages in any activity which is regarded as **art**. Most specifically, a painter; more generally, one who works in any field with refined dedication and distinction.

artists' frames

Types of picture frames so favoured by specific artists as to have become identified with them e.g. the **Watts** frame, named after George Frederick Watts (1817-1904). The interest of painters in the framing of their work reached its height in the latter half of the 19th century, largely due to the Pre-Raphaelites. John Downman (1750-1824) is another example with his characteristic neo-classical frame, also the American painter James McNeill Whistler (1834-1903), and the Englishmen Francis Cotes (1726-1770) and George Romney (1734-1802). *Vide* **country house frames**.

artist's proof

Trial impressions by a printmaker before printing, signed by the artist bottom left showing the individual number of each and the total number of artist's proofs the artist has signed, e.g. 7/10. When these are signed before an engraved title is introduced they are said to be 'before letters', the most sought after by collectors.

Artist's Resale Right

From February 2006 in the United Kingdom, living artists have been entitled to receive a resale royalty each time their work of a graphic or plastic kind protected by copyright is sold for the second or subsequent time. In order to qualify in the U.K. an artist must register with one of three officially recognised collecting agencies, and having done so cannot then legally waive his/her dues. Works sold for the first time are exempt, as are works for which copyright has expired, and those sold for less than the equivalent of 1,000 Euros. Current rates are a percentage

A

of the selling price on a sliding scale from 4% to 0.25%. Heirs of deceased artists whose work is protected by copyright may become eligible within the U.K. in 2012, although this is subject to confirmation.

Arts and Crafts Movement

A reformist British and North American movement in the decorative arts of the 19th and early 20th centuries. Inspired by the English designer and poet William Morris (1834-1896) and influenced historically by the earlier writings of the English critic John Ruskin (1819-1900), the English architect Augustus Pugin (1812-1852), and the French philosopher Jean-Jacques Rousseau (1719-1778). Its aim was to restore the art of craftsmanship at a time of increasing mechanisation. In 1861, Morris launched Morris & Co, inviting a group of craftsmen that included Dante Gabriel Rossetti (1828-1882) and Edward Burne-Jones (1833-1898), followed in 1890 by the Kelmscott Press with lasting influence on book design. Their aim was to create or promote hand-made objects and natural, phantasmagorical paintings.

Arundel prints

The *Arundel Society for Promoting the Knowledge of Art* (1848-1897) published about 200 line engravings and chromolithographs after Italian masters. The Society took its name after Thomas Howard, Earl of Arundel.

Ashcan School

A group of American social realist painters, active between 1905 and 1914 who sought in the first instance to bring attention to the slum conditions of New York. Largely influenced by Robert Henry (1865-1929) who sought to endow his art students with a social conscience. He initiated a group from which the Ashcan school developed.

ashlar

Smooth square-shaped stones used in buildings to face rougher work.

assay mark

A mark on gold and silver guaranteeing quality. In 1719 the lion passant was introduced as a device on silver indicating that the standard of 92.5% had been met.

astragal

A small, semi-circular moulding, round the top or bottom of a **column**. Copying classical architecture, the decoration often appeared as a string of **beads**, particularly when in association with **egg-and-dart moulding**.

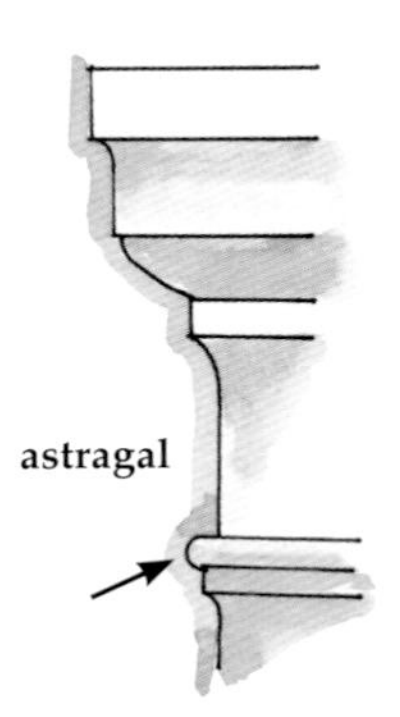

atrium

In Roman times this was the entrance hall and reception area, having the finest decoration in the building.

attribution

A term often diluted by auctioneers, galleries and art experts to denote the absence of certainty over the identity of an artist or designer. An unequivocal attribution denotes certainty but a work attributed to an artist suggests doubt. Most auction houses express degrees of probability: "a work catalogued with the name or recognised designation of an artist, without any qualification, is in our opinion, a work by the artist; 'attributed to' is in our opinion probably a work by the artist in whole or in part; 'studio of', 'workshop of', means in our opinion executed in the studio or workshop of the artist, possibly under his supervision; 'circle of', means in our opinion a work of the period of the artist and showing his influence; 'follower of' means in our opinion a work executed in the artist's style but not necessarily a pupil; 'manner of' indicates in our opinion a work executed in the artist's style but of a later date; 'after' in our opinion is a copy (of any date) of the artist." [*Christie's Explanation of Cataloguing Practice*].

Aubusson
Superior French tapestry from the eponymous town in central France. Believed to have originated with the arrival of Flemish weavers in the 16th century.

a(u)mbry
A small recess in a church wall; also a small cupboard for food and/or drink.

aureola
In Christian art, a halo of light depicted as surrounding the whole body of a divinity or **apostle**. When confined only to the head it is called a **nimbus**, which when painted in the shape of a square indicated the subject was still living.

auricular

auricular
A picture frame, common in the mid 17th century, with free flowing stylised organic forms, usually based upon animal or marine motifs.

autochrome
A 20th century application of lithographic stones used to colour a **monochrome** impression, the grain being excised from the block in order to provide highlights.

autotype
A photographic printing process first developed in 1883 to make print facsimiles using a carbon pigment. Also refers to a print made by the process.

avant-garde
The advance guard, the most progressive; often carrying uncertainty of lasting value; ahead of its time.

aventurin
A kind of **feldspar** used in the colouring of some glass and to give a golden glaze to porcelain. Sometimes called **sunstone**. Discovered accidentally in **Murano** when brass filings fell into a pot of molten glass. Also a form of sealing wax.

B

Baccarat

One of the two main types of fine French coloured crystal glass, made at the Baccarat factory, founded in 1778. Renowned for its magnificent paperweights. The best period was 1822-1858 when under the direction of Jean Baptiste Toussaint. Production ceased around 1870. *Vide* **Cristalleries de St-Louis**.

back edge

The outer edge of a frame, furthest from the image.

back frame

The structural part of the frame on to which carved **mouldings** may be fixed, often made of inferior wood. Also known as the **blind frame**.

badigeon

Several meanings depending on its use; in art it refers to a ground mix of plaster and stone used to repair small defects in a sculpture. Not to be confused with ***bodegón***.

baguette

An architectural term, used also in picture framing, for a small convex semi-circular moulding, the same as a **bead** without embellishment, and as a **chaplet** when adorned with foliage. In jewellery, a baguette is a gem in a long rectangular setting.

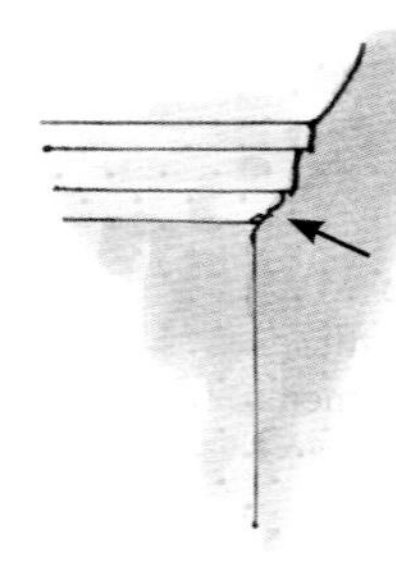

baguette

balance

A work of art is said to be 'balanced' when the design and the proportions of its components are evenly distributed. When the proportions are even it is said to be symmetrical, when uneven, it is said to be asymmetrical.

baldacchino

A canopy, fixed or portable, supported on columns, especially over altars, thrones, tombs, and papal conveyances. Also known as a BALDACHIN. From the Italian *baldacchino* describing something emanating from Baghdad, where brocade canopies were first made. Also called a **ciborium**.

baluster

An ornamental small pillar having a fanciful resemblance to the flower of a pomegranate. Also refers to the support for a railing or balustrade. BANISTER is a corrupt form of baluster of the latter type, now in more common use.

banding

Ornamental wooden bands decorating the edges of furniture.

Barbizon frame

A development of the 17th century Louis XIV frame, favoured by members of the **Barbizon School**. Characterised by a wide reverse **cove** with dense foliate decoration and an underlying subtle hatching giving the appearance of depth.

Barbizon frame

Barbizon School

A group of French landscape painters, led by Théodor Rousseau (1812-1867), who rebelled against classical convention, basing their work directly on nature. There was an emphasis on painting out of doors (***en plein air***), when the effects of the changing nuances of light could be captured most accurately. Other leading members of the group included Jean-François Millet (1814-1875), Charles Daubigny (1817-1878), Jules Dupré (1811-1889) and Narcisse Virgile Diaz (1807-1876). The name is derived from the village near Paris where they worked.

bard

Another word with different meanings. In Scotland it denotes a poet or singer; in heraldry it is the protective armour for a horse, when it can also be used as a verb.

bargeboard

bargeboard

Architectural term for a board placed on the face of a **gable**, underneath the BARGECOURSE (the roofing which projects beyond the rafters where there is a **gable**). Bargeboards first appeared in the 14th century. Also known as **gable-boards.**

baroque

A highly ornate, extravagant style in furniture and the decorative arts emerging between **mannerism** and **rococo**. Particularly associated with the Catholic counter-reformation and the reign of Louis XIV. In painting and sculpture its principal proponents were Giovanni Bernini (1598-1680), Michaelangelo Caravaggio (c1571-1610), Agostino Caracci (1557-1602), and Peter Paul Rubens (1557-1640). Sometimes known as the **Jesuit style** because of the unattractive architecture of many Jesuit churches. Baroque frames vary in type, all common in the 17th and early 18th centuries. They have in common naturalistic ornament repeated along most of their surfaces.

barrel vault

The plainest form of vaulting, generally built before the return of more complex groined vaulting in the 11th century.

barrel vault

bartizan

An overhanging turret.

basalt

A common volcanic rock, usually grey or black. BASALT WARE is a type of black stoneware developed by **Wedgwood**, also known as BLACK WARE.

base

In describing a frame, the bases are horizontal mouldings fitted beneath a **column**.

basilica

In classical Greece a **portico**, subsequently applied by the Romans to churches, public buildings, and mansions with **colonnades**.

bas relief

A sculpture or carving in which the **moulding** or carving projects very slightly from the ground or objects depicted. Also known as **low relief**.

bat printing

An overglaze process producing illustrations of great delicacy on to **porcelain**. Introduced in the 1760s. A design was printed in oil upon a sheet (a 'bat') made up of a mixture of glue, treacle and whiting, the outline being transferred on to the ware, dusted with the chosen colour, the surplus then being removed with cotton wool. Special paper replaced the use of a bat c1825.

Batik

Originating in Java, a method of producing

coloured textile designs, using molten wax and coloured die.

Bauhaus

A school of design initiated by the architect Walter Gropius (1883-1969) at Weimar in 1919. The propelling impulse was the need for collective work, particularly in architecture, to improve the quality of life. This implied simple design, often related to industrial technology. In painting, the leading figures were the abstract artist Wassily Kandinsky (1866-1944), who left his native Russia to join the Bauhaus group as head of mural painting, the delicate art of Paul Klee (1879-1940), who constantly experimented with different materials, and Josef Albers (1888-1976), responsible for craft teaching within the group 1923-5. The school was closed by Hitler in 1933 when most of the teachers emigrated, many to the United States where the Bauhaus philosophy attained international influence, especially in architecture.

Baxter print

First developed by George Baxter (1804-1867), the father of colour printing. The process, patented in 1835, involved an initial metal keyplate and a block for each colour, all produced on hand presses.

bead

In architecture and joinery it refers to an ornament making a junction or separation between the shaft and **capital** of a **column**. *Vide* **baguette**.

bead-and-reel

An embellishment in the form of a thin, convex **moulding** with alternating circular and elliptical or elongated motifs, the beads generally in twos or threes. Various forms may be distinguished, for example BEAD-AND-BUTT (where the panel is flush with the framing, with a bead running on two plain edges); **return-bead** (where the angle of the bead is relieved on both surfaces); BEAD, BUTT AND SQUARE WORK (a panel with beads on one side only); BEAD, FLUSH AND SQUARE (beaded on only one side).

beauty

A quality in an object or view that pleases the eye of the beholder to the extent that it arouses the use of the adjective 'beautiful', which, like colour, can only be described in terms of itself. It may be distinguished from the SUBLIME, the emotion, for example, aroused by a view of the Himalaya mountains, in that the sublime excites a feeling of awe. It has long been debated whether value judgements are invariably subjective or whether objective standards are possible. To those who favour the former view, the ascription of beauty to an object or natural landscape is intuitive, lying beyond argument. To those favouring the latter view the ascription of beauty will vary for an individual as experience and taste overcome intuition and the constraints of fashion. Kant, in his *Critique of Aesthetic Judgement*, argued that aesthetic judgements can claim universal validity but 'proofs are of no avail whatsoever for determining the judgement of taste'.

B

He distinguished between what he called 'free beauty' and 'dependent beauty'. Free beauty is when it is attributed to an individual or object, and dependent beauty is when an object is considered beautiful of its kind. There is also, he believed, a difference between judgement of taste and judgement of the agreeable, the former being *disinterested*, the latter *interested*. Another significant difference was identified by Ruskin who distinguished the response to sensual pleasure (*aesthesis*) from the response of one's moral being (*theoria*). The relationship of beauty to **art** is complex.

Beaux-Arts
An elaborate classical style of the late 19th and early 20th centuries, referring to the rules and teachings of the Ecole des Beaux-Arts in Paris.

bed-molding
A molding of the **cornice** of an **entablature**. In classical buildings it is situated beneath the **corona** and above the **frieze**; similarly in picture frames.

beetle damage
Vide **woodworm**.

bellarmine
A large stoneware jug decorated with the face of a bearded and corpulent man. Originally a caricature of a Cardinal Bellarmine who opposed the reformation.

Belleek china
A form of white **parian** china originating in Fermanagh in 1857. Belleek ware is still made there.

belle epoque
The period of quiet unhurried life characteristic of Edwardian times, ending in 1914.

bema
A pulpit or raised place for addressing an assembly. Also refers to a step of approximately two and a half feet used by Greeks and others of the time as a measure in the building of a stadium or similar construction.

Ben Day medium
An esoteric, largely obsolete procedure whereby a grain or shading medium is applied to a drawing before being photographed, often for colour reproduction. The name is taken from the American Ben Day who in 1883 transferred patterned gelatin for inking onto an original design.

bergère
An easy chair, generously upholstered,

designed more for comfort than for decoration.

bestiary
A medieval illuminated book that used animals, real or mythical, to provide moral injunctions.

bezant
An historical term describing a gold or silver coin originally minted in Byzantium. In heraldry it denotes a gold plate, or flat piece of gold with no impression upon it.

bicranium
An ornament in the form of an ox skull, usually in **low relief**. Also called a BUCRANIUM.

Biedermeier
A decorative style of design popular in Germany during the first half of the 19th century. Commonly ascribed to clean-lined furniture but also to a style in architecture, literature and music. Paralleled by the Regency style in Britain and the French Empire style, of which it was a simplified version.

bifora
Twin-arch, as in some church windows. Hence a BIFORATE window is one with two openings, often with a roundel above. Also known as a VENETIAN ARCH.

bijouterie
Minor jewellery.

birthstone
Precious stones have been ascribed to calendar months. Thus January-garnet; February-amethyst; March-aquamarine; April-diamond; May-emerald; June-pearl; July-ruby; August-peridot (olivine); September-sapphire; October-opal; November-citrine/topaz; December-turquoise/zircan.

bisque
In pottery, bisque ware is the product of the first firing of the kiln. It also refers to an unglazed white **porcelain** used in the making of statuettes.

bister
A brown pigment extracted from wood (preferably beech) soot. Often used in early watercolour drawings for applying tints before **India ink** came into use.

bitumen
A tar-like black substance, a mixture of asphaltum and drying oil, used by some oil painters in the 19th century. It is resistant to removal and therefore to cleaning and restoration.

blanc-de-chine
A type of fine white Chinese **porcelain** from the mid 14th century onward. The delicate characteristic whiteness is due to the reduced use of iron oxide, making the firing to a warm white tone in an oxidising atmosphere possible without recourse to great heat.

Blaureiter school
Co-founded in Munich in 1911 by the Russian abstract artist Wassily Kandinsky

(1866-1944). Named after the eponymous work called in English *The Blue Rider*. The school may be regarded as a phase in the development of **Expressionism**. At its height it was a multi-national group including the Russian Alexei von Jawlensky (1864-1941), the Swiss Paul Klee (1879-1940), the Germans Franz Marc (1880-1916) and August Mücke (1887-1914), and the Frenchman Robert Delauney (1885-1961). The school epitomised the intense use of colour and abstract form.

blind frame
Vide **back frame**.

bloom
Cloudiness on the surface of a painting produced by miniscule cracks through which light is diffused.

bodegón
Derived from the Spanish for wine cellar, it came to describe pictures of kitchen scenes.

Body art
An artistic development of the mid 20th century in which the human body became the medium, whether through paint, disfigurement or mutilation.

body colour
The use of pigment in works of art, especially watercolours, to provide accentuated colour and opacity.

bole
A soft, compact, oily clay used as a fixative for **gold leaf**. Various forms of clay have been used, pale red Armenian bole used as an absorbent and astringent; yellow bole of Blois which effervesces when mixed with acid; Bohemian bole has a yellow flaky texture making it difficult to use; French bole is another pale red variety with tints of yellow and white; Lemnian bole is also pale red; Silesian bole is yellow and sometimes used medicinally.

bolection
A little used term to describe a **raffle leaf frame**. Introduced in the late 17th century, it has a distinctive convex or **ogee** moulding of reverse section curving up from the picture and back to the wall. The term is most common in joinery where it refers to a **moulding** which projects beyond the surface it decorates.

bolection

bombé
A piece of furniture or ornament shaped like a dome.

bone china
A kind of **porcelain** midway between hard and soft paste; a combination of china clay and china stone strengthened and whitened with calcified bone.

bonheur de jour

bonheur de jour

Desks of varied designs, popular in France in the mid 18th century. Typically, it is a small cabinet with a writing box and extended flap. Panels came to be painted in the 1860s, often with **Wedgwood bas reliefs** or simulated **Sèvres**.

bordure

An archaic term for a border, still used in heraldry where it refers to the border of a shield.

botryoid

Having the appearance and shape of a bunch of grapes.

bouillotte lamp

A four-arm candleholder with an adjustable metal shade and a dished base for holding game tokens. Developed in the late 18th century for use during the French gambling card game 'bouillotte'.

bouillotte lamp

boule

Material, usually brass or tortoiseshell, used to make decorative inlays, especially **marquetry**. The French first introduced this form of decoration led by the furniture designer A. C. Boule (1642-1732).

box frame

Modern synonym for a **Cassetta frame**, having a flat section bordered by raised inner and outer **mouldings**.

brass

A durable alloy of copper and zinc differing from bronze in its greater proportion of zinc. Beating brass plates to extreme thinness produces brass leaf otherwise known as **Dutch leaf** or **Dutch gold**.

brayer

A kind of small composition roller used in printmaking for applying ink to printing surfaces.

brigantine

brigantine

A sailing vessel often depicted in coastal and estuarial paintings of the 18th and 19th centuries, having two masts, the foremost square-rigged. It was used primarily for trading purposes and thus a popular target for brigands. In heraldry, a brigantine is a coat of mail.

Britannia device
In 1696 the conversion of silver coin into plate caused an Act to be passed raising the standard of wrought plate from 925 parts of pure silver per thousand to 958 parts. The marks of the leopard's head and lion passant were withdrawn and substituted by the figure of Britannia with the lion's head erased. This remained compulsory until 1720, becoming optional thereafter.

Britannia metal
A type of **pewter** containing no lead, making it more suitable for eating and drinking utensils.

Britannia silver
Silver which is at least 95.8% pure.

bronze
Two meanings. An **alloy** of most parts copper to smaller parts of tin. For statuaries the proportion of tin varies from 1% to 25%. Since the mid 1870s a very small percentage of phosphorus has been introduced giving a finer grain and longer life. A bronze can also refer to an object made in bronze, whether cast or wrought.

bronze disease
A formation of bright green porous spots on bronze caused by salts found in the soil. The spots, known as bronze disease, although seriously corrosive, can be easily cured by a skilled restorer.

bronze powder
Pulverised bronze, mixed with a painting medium, used to renovate **gilded** wood. The copper in the bronze leads to oxidisation and darkening.

bronzes d'ameublement
French term with no English equivalent for furniture made of bronze, patinated or gilt.

brush etching
Vide **foul-biting**.

brushes
Artists' paint brushes are known by their respective shapes. The most common are (i) BRIGHTS, flat and square-edged; (ii) FILBERTS, flat, oval-edged with a long fibre; (iii)FLATS, square-edged with an extended bristle; (iv) LONGS, also flat and square-edged with a long sable; and (v) ROUNDS, with a pointed bristle.

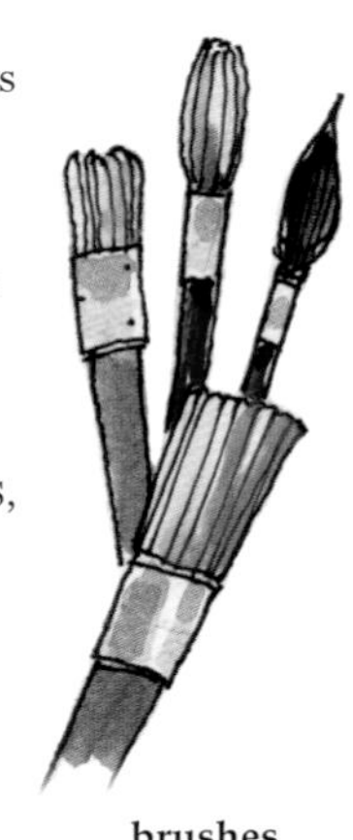

brushes

bucranium
Vide **bicranium**.

buffet
A term applied to various forms of furniture, originally with tiered shelves, for displaying precious objects. The predecessor of the **double corner cupboard**.

buffet stool
Vide **tabouret**.

bunched leaf

Type of **baroque frame** dating from the late 17th century decorated with a repeated pattern of bunched leaves, often hanging from an ornamental rope. Oak leaves were the most common to be copied.

bureau

A desk or writing table with drawers. An **escritoire**.

burin

The main cutting tool of a line engraver. This has an obliquely pointed head of various shapes. The handle is pressed in to the engraver's palm for cutting with a strong pushing motion. Also known as a **graver**.

burin

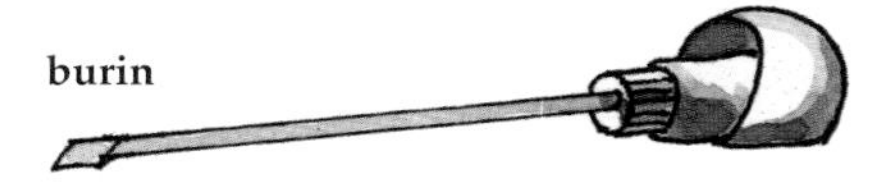

burlap

A coarse cloth used for wrapping and in upholstery.

burnisher

A tool used by etchers and frame makers to polish by rubbing, usually having smooth, slightly curved polished sides and a rounded point. Wood engravers use the tool for taking a trial proof by hand; the inked raised lines are placed over a sheet of **India paper** and, by using a burnisher evenly across the surface, obtain a precise impression.

burnisher

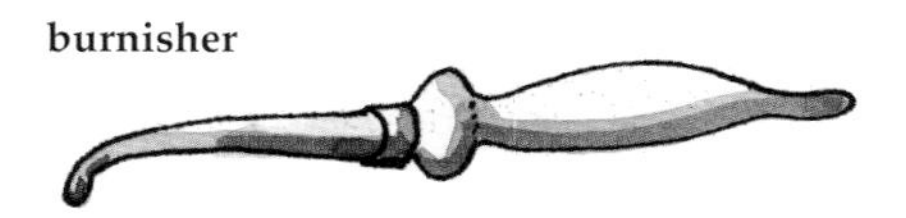

burnishing

The use of the burnisher to polish **water gilding**.

burr

The rough edge left on metal or paper after it has been punched or cut.

butt joint

A wooden joint connecting two closely abutting members. Known also as a BUTTING or ABUTTING JOINT.

butterfly key

A key shaped like a butterfly used on the back of a frame to secure a **mitre joint**.

buttress

A support for an external wall, also called a **counterfort**. A **flying buttress** is a support in the form of a segment of an arch springing from a solid wall or pillar and abutting another part of the structure. A **hanging buttress** is a buttress not standing on

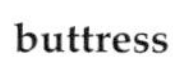

a foundation but supported by a **corbel**, chiefly as a decoration.

Byzantine

A style of decorative art enjoyed in the Eastern Roman Empire stemming from the addition of oriental detail upon classic styles, leading to the debasement of the latter. Byzantian architecture is the prototype of the **Norman** and **Saxon** style. As an adjective it describes a composition or design of extremely complicated detail.

Byzantine mosaic

Vide **mosaic**.

C

cabinet miniature
Vide **miniatures**.

cabling
A term used in framing to describe an ornamental device with concave **channels** having convex fillings in the lower part of their concavities, reminiscent of a rope.

cabochon
Most commonly this refers to a **gem** polished but not faceted. If cut without **facets**, rounded and convex on top and flat, concave on the back, the stone is said to be *en cabochon*. In framing the term is used to describe an egg within a circular surround, often in a patterned series separated by a leaf or **dart**. Used as **top-edged** ornament in some mid 18th century frames.

cabriole
A curved leg on a piece of furniture. Common in the designs of Thomas Chippendale and during the Queen Anne period.

cacotechny
A bad or corrupt state of art.

cadenas
A casket, with lock and key, placed on the table to house the eating utensils of an important person. Common in the middle ages, often in the form of a ship. During the Renaissance they were usually oblong.

cadency, marks of
Bearings in an armorial shield distinguishing branches of a family.

caduceus
A herald's staff. In classical mythology specifically, the wand carried by Hermes, or Mercury, the latter indicating authority, quality, and office. Originally it was a plain rod entwined with strands of wool. This changed to serpents and then to winged serpents. More recently, Mercury being the god of commerce, the caduceus represents power (the rod), wisdom (the serpent), and diligence (the wings).

caduceus

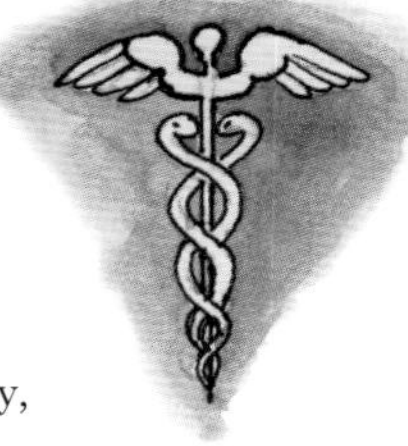

C

caelevit
Vide **sculpt**.

caisson
A sunken panel on some frames and in some Renaissance buildings. In architecture it is in the ceiling. Also (a) a sealed compartment for working underwater, and (b) an ammunition chest or wagon.

calabash
A dried hollowed-out gourd for holding drinking liquid.

calamander
A close-grained ebony wood used in making furniture. From the Asian tree *Diospyros qualsita*.

calf
Leather from the hide of a calf used for bookbinding. It can be variously treated so as to produce DICED, MARBLED, MOTTLED, SCORED, SPRINKLED, or TREE CALF.

calotype
A photographic negative with light and shadow reversed. Invented by the English photographer William Fox Talbot (1800-1877) in 1839. A process, no longer used, whereby a reflected image was impressed on sensitised paper by exposure in a camera and developed by gallonitrate of silver, fixed by hyposulphite of soda. Also known as a **talbotype**.

cameo
A small piece of hard stone, often onyx, carved in **relief** on a different coloured background. In framing it denotes a small oval decoration, often in a **frieze**. When cut on stone they are called **stone cameos**, when cut in shells they are **shell cameos**, with colours varying according to the kind of shell.

cameo glass
A convex glass used in the mounting of hand-painted photographs or other images.

cameotype
An early name for a small vignette **daguerrotype** mounted in a jewelled setting.

cameo ware
Fine pottery with figures in **relief**, a speciality of the firm **Wedgwood**.

camera lucida
An instrument for reflecting an image by means of a prism on to a flat surface. Its main use was in viewing images obtained microscopically.

camera obscura
A darkened box or larger enclosed space

incorporating a lens with an aperture for projecting an image of a distant object on to a screen. The procedure became popular with artists in the 18th century, particularly with Giovanni Canaletto (1697-1768). The eye is another example.

campaign
A term in the art trade referring to work undertaken on a painting by a restorer. Hence, for example, an old master painting will probably have undergone a number of campaigns, i.e. work undertaken at different times.

campana
The bell shaped core of a **Corinthian capital**. Campana is Spanish for a bell so that the term refers in general to any bell shaped object. CAMPANA RELIEF is a Roman terracotta relief panel, named after the Italian collector Giampietro Campana (1808-1880).

campanile
A bell tower.

canted
Any surface which is bevelled, **chamfered** or obliquely faced.

canterbury
Furniture with slatted partitions for holding books, music and papers.

cantilever
A metal or wooden arm projecting from a wall to support a balcony or similar structure.

canvas
Coarse cloth most often made from flax or hemp, used as a surface for painting in oils. More loosely it can also refer to a completed work, excluding the frame. May be sold in rolls, stretched on frames, or in panels. There are several types: **sail cloth**, or especially woven fabric of four kinds known respectively as SINGLE PRIME, SMOOTH, ROMAN, or TWILLED.

capital
The ornament on top of a **column** or pillar, often in the form of a scroll. There are five orders of architecture each with their distinctive type of column. In order of their appearance they are: **Doric**, **Ionic**, **Corinthian**, **Tuscan** and **Composite**.

Capo di Monte
A kind of **porcelain**, generally table-ware, first produced at the Palace of Capo di Monte in Italy in the mid 18th century. Often in the form of figures on a white ground with vivid coloured **rococo** decorations. The castle is also famed for its fine collection of European paintings.

capriccio
A picture of a fantastical or highly unusual character.

carat
Unit of measurement indicating the amount of gold in an object. Originally, a carat was the twenty-fourth part. Thus pure gold is 24 carats. One carat is 200 milligrams, and one hundredth of that is called a **point**. Also a unit to describe **precious stones**.

caricature

From the Latin for exaggeration, an image of a person or thing in which coarseness and defects are exaggerated and finer points neglected, for the purpose of satire.

Carlo

Synonymous with **Acanthus-and-Tongue**, a commonly used embellishment to the hollow or **sight edge** of a **Carlo Maratta frame**.

Carlo Maratta frame

A common type of frame with a prominent curved **top edge**, derived from the design of the Italian baroque painter Carlo Maratta (1625-1713). Popular in Britain in the late 17th century. Often enriched with **acanthus leaves** in the depth of the front hollow or along the **sight edge**. Particularly popular among portrait painters. Maratta frames fell from general favour in the 1790s, but enjoyed a revival in the 19th century. Also known as a **Salvador Rosa** frame.

Carlton House furniture

Type of furniture design, typically a desk or writing table, common in the 1790s and during the Regency period. Characterised by a D-shaped top, with the sitter facing the straight rather than the curved side and with the superstructure surrounding the curve, flanking the writing space.

carolean

Of or pertaining to the reign of Charles II (1660-1685). Not to be confused with CAROLINGIAN, i.e. associated with the reign of Charlemagne (748-814).

cartoon

A preliminary drawing of a design for a painting or other work of art. Generally done on rough paper of similar size to the planned finished work. Can also refer to a **caricature** or symbolic composition intended to provoke or attack a political or social idea or person(s).

cartouche

A scroll-like ornament which may appear as the **volute** of an **Ionic capital**. Also used in early maps when it refers to a tablet imitating a scroll within which is an inscription or illustration. In heraldry, it is the English term for the oval **escutcheon** found in Italian ecclesiastical use.

carving

Producing a shape by cutting in to a hard material. A branch of sculpture of a decorative type rather than of monumental relief or statuary.

caryatid

The statue of a woman dressed in long robes, placed as a **column** or pillar to support a larger structure. Women thus dressed in architecture and sculpture are said to be in the CARYATIC manner. A decorative feature in some furniture designs.

cassappanca

A wooden bench above a built-in chest. When the **cassone** lost its popularity, the cassappanca survived as a useful accessory, especially for an entrance hall.

cassetta
A frame consisting of a simple, **lap-jointed** back frame and entablature-derived mouldings. Italian name for an internationally popular frame with mixed inner and outer mouldings; also known as a **box frame**.

cassolettes
Vide **censer**.

cassone
A large chest, often richly decorated. Originally used in Italy during the middle ages to hold the more valuable parts of a bridal equipment.

castellated
Castle-like, with turrets and battlements.

catacomb
Underground burial chamber.

catalogue raisonné
A complete list of an artist's work (as known to the compiler), generally annotated with a description and comments.

Caucasian
Vide **Oriental carpets**.

cauliculus
In early frames, an **acanthus** or lotus leaf surrounding the **fillet** of a **volute**. From the archaeological term describing one of the lesser branches in a characteristic **Corinthian capital**, sprouting from the CAULES or main stalks which support the **volutes**, distinguished from the main stalks themselves from which they emerge.

cavetto
A quarter-circle concavity found in some frames. May refer to any hollow or recessed pattern, the reverse of **relief**. *In cavetto* means any design, impressed or stamped, differing from **intaglio** because not incised by a sharp instrument. When the field is recessed, with a design in relief upon it, it is known as a CAVORILIEVO.

Celadon
Chinese pottery with a pale gray-greenish glaze which became a favourite at **Sèvres**. Also refers to the colour itself.

cella
Vide **pronaos**.

cel(l)aret(te)
A furniture cabinet for holding wine bottles. Unlike a **wine cooler**, a cellaret or **garde-de-vin**, has a lid, is compartmentalised, and lockable.

censer
A vessel for burning incense and perfume. Also called a **thurible**. The openings through which the vapours appear are called **cassolettes**.

centaur
A mythological beast first introduced with

the head and torso of a man and a horse's hindquarters behind, but this combination was abandoned in favour of the chest and arms of a human and the body and legs of a horse.

centre-and-corner

Refers to an early 18th century frame with prominent centre and corner motifs.

ceramic(s)

Any object made from clay hardened by heat. This may be **earthenware**, **porcelain** or **stoneware**, depending on the method of production.

chain carving

An **ovolo** or **torus moulding**, carved in imitation of the interlocking links of a chain.

chalcedony

A kind of quartz first found at Chalcedon in Ancient Greece. In colour it resembles slightly clouded milk with circles, spots, or veins. Varieties include **chrysoprase**, **sand**, and **sardonyx**. Also known as **white agate**.

chalk roll(er)

The cutting tool aimed at simulating the surface texture of strokes of chalk in processing the crayon, or chalk, type of line engraving. This gives an irregular grain appropriate to this type of etching.

chamfer

A sloping or bevelled surface cut along the edge of a frame, panel, or occasionally along the margins of a book cover. Also a verb.

chancel

The enclosed area surrounding the altar and separated from the **choir**. In Courts of Justice it is the space railed off between the presiding official(s) and the rest of the court.

channel

A flattened concave **moulding** similar to a **scotia** but less deep.

chaplet

Vide **baguettes**.

charcoal

A kind of crayon used for drawing, usually in the form of a stick. Although producing a strong line it is liable to smudging. Charcoal is a black residue from wood or bone heated in airless conditions.

charge

In heraldry, a device or figure borne on the shield on a coat of arms. Ancient charges were simpler than modern examples so that a shield only divided in to a few compartments is likely to be older than one charged with a large number of devices.

charka

Russian liquid measurement corresponding to 123 ml. Hence, also a small drinking vessel, varying in decoration according to period, in silver or rich enamel.

chase

In the field of art it has two distinct meanings. The more common is a verb meaning to emboss or to engrave a metal.

In printing, a chase is the metal frame enclosing the composed type.

chatelaine
A Western adornment worn at a lady's waist, a derivative from the French *châtelaine*, the female custodian of a castle who wore a girdle around her waist to which the keys would be attached.

cherub
An angel of the second celestial order. Usually depicted as a winged young child.

chevron
Any V-shaped ornament, line or stripe.

chiaroscuro
The distribution of light and shade in a picture; the combined effect of all its lights, reflections and shadows.

chiffonier
A portable cupboard with a sideboard top; a cabinet suited to the morning room. *Vide* **commode**.

chiffonier

china
The common name for **porcelain**, nowadays extended to encompass all kinds of ceramic tableware.

china clay
Vide **soapstone porcelain**.

china stone
Weathered felspathic granite, ground to a fine powder giving hard-paste **porcelain** its vitreous quality.

C

Chinese carpets
Vide **Oriental carpets**.

Chinese emblems
Certain symbols frequently appear in Chinese art. The eight Buddhist emblems are: THE WHEEL, THE PARASOL, THE CANOPY, THE LOTUS-FLOWER (the holy flower of Buddha), THE CONCH, THE VASE HOLDING THE WATER OF LIFE, TWO FISH, and the EVERLASTING KNOT. There are also eight Taoist symbols: THE SWORD, THE GOURD AND CRUTCH, THE LOTUS-FLOWER, THE FLUTE, THE BAMBOO TUBE & MAGIC WAND, THE FAN, THE CASTANETS, and THE FLOWER BASKET.

chinoiserie
A decorative style, imitating the Chinese, particularly in ceramics and furniture.

Chippendale
An elegant style of furniture, first designed by Thomas Chippendale (1718-1779).

chisel
A hand tool with a bevelled cutting edge used for shaping metal and wood.

choir
Portion of the interior of a church, east of the **nave**, for the use of the singers.

chroma
The intensity or purity of a **colour**.

C

chromascope
A video synthesiser of **colour** that produces moving coloured abstract patterns and images that, when transferred on to computer software, can be used for amusement or design purposes.

chromolithography
A method of obtaining coloured **lithographic** pictures by using prepared lithographic stones. When finished, the prints are passed through an embossing press to give a canvaslike effect.

chuprassy
Badge of office, usually attached to the belt. Can also refer to a messenger, someone carrying a cuprassy, identifying the office from which he comes. Also called a CHAPRAS.

cibachrome
A process of art colour printing producing images of the finest quality. This uses a chemically inert polyester base so that the colours do not fade. The dyes used are of top quality. Known also as **ilfrachrome classic print**.

ciborium
Vide **baldacchino**.

cinnabar
A heavy bright red mineral. Vermilion. Also a red juice obtained from the East Indian tree *Calamus draco*. *Vide* **dragon's blood**.

cinque-foil
A flower with five petals, frequently used in heraldic **charges**. In architecture, and sometimes on frames, it is any five-cusped ornamentation.

cire perdu
An early method of casting **bronze** by making a model in wax and enclosing it in plaster, melting the wax out of the plaster, then using the latter as a mould for the bronze.

citrine
A lemon colour, the first of the tertiary group of colours or ultimate compound of the three: yellow, red and blue. It also refers to a yellow, pellucid type of **quartz**, often called **false topaz**.

cladding
Material protecting an exterior surface. One common wooden example is a CLAPBOARD.

clasp

clasp
A flat leaf motif clasping or surrounding the centre or corner of a frame, most frequently on frames of the mid 17th century.

classical
A term used loosely denoting either a work reminiscent of classical antiquity or of exemplary standard. The former use is to be preferred.

Classical Realism
An American movement of the late 20th century which sought a return to classical techniques and the creation of the beautiful as an antidote to **modern art**.

clay
An essential ingredient in the making of all **ceramics**. It is a firm, sticky type of earth, formed by the decomposition and consequent hydration of feldspathic rocks, most often gneiss, granite or other crystalline rocks. The purest types are all refractory, known as **china-clay**, **fine-clay** or **kaolinite-clay**.

clepsydra
A machine for recording time by the passage of water through a small aperture.

clerestory (clearstorey)
The windowed upper storey of a church, above the **triforium** (if any).

cliché
The duplication of an engraving by electrolysis. This provides a near perfect replica. Thus cliché casting is casting produced by forcing the mould quickly on to melted metal.

cloison
The **fillet** used in the making of **cloisonné**. A dividing band of **ivory** forming a white outline which sets off the brilliance of the coloured stones.

cloisonné
An enamel finish obtained by an area of different colours separated by **fillets** of wire positioned edgeways on to a metal or porcelain backing. The interstices or cells between the metal strips are filled with enamel paste of suitable colours vitrified by heat. The surface is then ground until smooth and polished.

cloisonné mosaic
A decorative artistic pattern in which dividing lines, ridges or bars are prominent, the spaces between being filled with coloured material, generally glass.

cloister
An arched walkway round the walls of colleges and monasteries.

clouté d'or
Vide **piqué**.

CMYK
For use in four colour printing, the letters stand for cyan, magenta, yellow and black. Refers also to the process itself, technically known as subtractive because the ink removes ('subtracts') brightness from the white background. *Vide* **Pantone**.

coffer
An architectural term for a sunken ornamental panel in a roof. Also refers, when describing a frame, to a rosette traditionally surrounded by four lengths of **taenia** moulding. Another meaning

describes a large wooden chest for storing objects of value such as money or jewels.

C

cognescenti

Vide **connoisseur**.

collage

An artistic procedure in which a variety of materials, generally fabric, paint, paper or wood, or a mixture of any of these, are arranged and then glued to a backing. The most common applications are of paper or wood.

collation

Term commonly used by bookmen to indicate **format**, the register of signatures (letters printed in the tail margin of each **gathering**) and the number of pages. Sometimes used by printsellers to show that a print has been compared and found similar to a known copy in all particulars, especially concerning the width of margin which for early etchings can be vital in determining age and issue.

collet

A band or collar. As a jewelry term a CULET is the flat surface below a gem, also known as a CULLET, COLLET or **lower table**. In armory it refers to that part protecting the back of the body from the waist down. In glass-making, a collet is that part of an object which adheres to the **pontil**.

Collins frame

A frame having a prominent **cushion**, with a running ornamental foliage pattern, often with wide, flat shell or scroll corners. Most common in the mid 19th century. Probably so-called after the under-rated English landscape painter William Collins (1788-1847) who favoured this type of frame for his own work.

collotype

Printing term referring to a print made by exposing a thin sheet of gelatine to light and then treated with a substance to produce an image. Most frequently used after 1868 when the quality of gelatine improved.

colonnade

A row of **columns**, usually supporting a roof.

colophon

A note at the end of a book giving details of the work e.g. author, publisher, date of publication. The nature of the details may vary.

colophony

A dark brown resin used in the making of cheaper grades of **varnish**. Obtained from distilling crude turpentine with water.

colour

The visual sensation produced by light upon an object or view, varying according to different wavelengths, ranging from violet which has the highest frequency and shortest wavelength to red which has the lowest frequency and longest wavelength. The average person sees six colours: red, orange, green, yellow, blue and violet.

One person in several thousand can distinguish seven colours in the spectrum while about 20% of the population has diminished perception and between 3% and 4% of the population is colour-blind. Every colour has five qualities: **hue** (tint), **tonal value**, **chroma** (degree of brilliance), **temperature** (e.g. red and yellow are warm and appear to come toward the observer, blue and violet are cold and appear to recede from the viewer), and **transparency** (degree of opacity). **Primary colours** (red, blue and green) can be mixed to produce almost any colour. In printing, because the mixture of pigments depends on the wavelengths absorbed, the **primary colours** are different, being magenta, cyan (a greenish blue), and yellow.

colour collotype

A **collotype** made with difficulty by using colour filters on separate negatives, printed with a grey keyplate.

colour fast

Material with colours that will not fade because of the dye or paint used.

colour field

In the 20th century some abstract painters concentrated on large areas of undifferentiated colour (the colour field) to the exclusion of form.

colourist

A term applied in **modern art** to a painter who gives the use of colour and the treatment of light pre-eminence over form or substance. Specifically, outside the French Impressionists, the best known are the four leading so-called Scottish Colourists: Samuel John Peploe (1871-1935), John Duncan Fergusson (1874-1961), George Leslie Hunter (1877-1931), and Francis Cadell (1883-1937).

column

Derived from the architectural term, when describing a **tabernacle frame** it refers to the middle circular support, generally with a **capital** on top and a base at the foot.

comb scraper

A tool with an extended serrated edge and a long handle used by coppersmiths for smoothing copper.

commission

A variable figure charged to vendors by an artist, auction house or art gallery for services rendered. The figure varies significantly and is usually returnable if the object is subsequently withdrawn. Also refers to a purchasing order given to an artist for proposed work or to a buyer's agent for bidding at auction.

commode

A type of bedside table for a chamber pot. More generally, since 1760 it refers to a chest of drawers with a top suitable for refined ornamentation. A portable table or chest of drawers with a sideboard top is more correctly termed a **chiffonier**, although the term commode is now widely used to denote any chest of drawers.

C

complementary colours
Colours which when mixed together make black or white. They are arranged opposite each other on a colour wheel: red and green, blue and orange, yellow and purple.

compo(sition)
A mixture usually made of glue, linseed oil, resin and whiting which when mixed is used to make a moulded ornament. Composition also refers to the subject of a drawing or painting.

composite
The fifth (latest) type of classical (Roman) architecture which comprised elements of both the **Corinthian** and the **Ionic** orders. The **capital** was borrowed from the **Tuscan**, ranks of leaves from the **Corinthian**, and **volutes** from the **Ionic**.

composuit
Vide **inven(it)**.

conceptual art
An artistic approach in which a concept is regarded as more important than the completed work. Typically, examples take the form of large paintings, photographs or even videos. It has been described as anti-art and can be traced back to the influence of the French painter Marcel Duchamp (1887-1968).

connoisseur
An expert in the discernment of quality of a particular art form, style or period. ***Cognoscenti*** is an occasionally used synonym.

console
An ornamented bracket support shaped in an **S-scroll**, with the ends of differing widths.

Constructivism
An art movement involving sculpture, originating in Russia in the 1920s. Industrial materials such as glass, metal, perspex, or wire, are used to give an angular, often abstract and three dimensional image in paintings, simulating sculpture. The aim was to incorporate the concepts of time and movement in to sculpture. Principle proponents were the sculptors Naum Gabo (1890-1977) and Antoine Pevsner (1886-1962).

conté
A kind of pencil. A substitute for lead pencil first developed by the French artist and soldier Nicolas-Jacques Conté (1755-1805). Napoleon asked Conté to fabricate a pencil without lead as import of the latter had been restricted. He achieved this by pressing powdered graphite and clay between a pair of wooden cylinders. Usually black or red.

copper plate
Used by engravers. In the 18th century this would be polished with various stones, **charcoal** and a steel **burnisher** rendering the finished product flat and free from all indentations. The introduction of hard steel c1820 produced a significant improvement.

copy
An umbrella term denoting that an image is either an imitation of an original

or a later version. The former may or may not indicate clandestine work, the latter does not. In printing, copy refers to material, generally a text, ready for publication. *Vide* **cliché**, **fake**, **forgery**, **pastiche**, **plagiarism**.

coquillage
Carved ornament in the shape of a shell, particularly associated with the **rococo** style characteristic in the reign of Louis XV. From the French word *coquille* (shellfish).

corbel
A piece of metal or stone projecting from a wall to support an object above. Corbels come in many different shapes and decorations.

cordage
Vide **paper**.

Corinthian
Relating to Corinth, in architecture the Corinthian order is the most ornate and slender of the classical orders. The **capital** is bell-shaped, adorned with **acanthus leaves**, with a generally concave **abacus** supported by graceful **volutes**. There is a Corinthian style in pottery as well as in picture framing.

Corinthian

corner block
A block used on the back of a frame to secure a **mitre joint** and the inner and back frame. Common in the 19th century.

cornice
An ornamental **moulding** round the upper wall of a room; a group of raised mouldings on the topside of an **entablature**.

cornucopia
A goat's horn surrounded by a wreath symbolising concord, peace and plenty. The term is applied to any object similarly shaped.

corona
In frames, this refers to an overhanging **moulding** at the top of a **cornice** between the **bed-moulding** and the **cymatium**.

coronation mark
A mark incised on silver bearing the head of Queen Elizabeth II to commemorate the year of her accession (1953).

couchant
A recumbent figure with an uplifted head.

counterfeit
As a verb, to imitate an object without authority. As a noun, an object made to deceive or defraud.

counterfort
Vide **buttress**.

counterproof
A proof taken not from the plate but from a paper impression while the ink remains

moist. Such proofs are of no value being used only to enable the engraver to make additions or revisions.

C

Counter Reformation

Reform of the Roman Catholic Church from within led by the Jesuits, highlighted at the Council of Trent (1545-1563). The effects on the graphic arts, other than on religious art, were minimal.

country house frames

Many of the finest frames in Britain during the 17th and 18th centuries came to be associated with the aristocratic dynasties who sponsored their own favourite types. Among the most distinguished examples were the homes of the 1st Duke of Lauderdale and Earls of Dysart (Ham House), the 9th Duke of Norfolk (Arundel Castle, removed from the old Norfolk house in London's Mayfair), the Earls of Berkeley (Berkeley Castle), and the Marquesses of Hertford (Hertford House, now the Wallace Collection in London).

cove

A small **hollow**. An architectural term also used in framing. The REVERSE COVE is an example seen in the outer ornamentation of a **Barbizon frame** where the ornamented surface emerges in a gentle rise from a flat inner area, creating a small hollow at its outset.

coving

An arched projection on a building.

crackle glazes

Vide **crazing**.

craquelure

Small cracks in a canvas caused by age and the loss of paint. Paint loss can generally be made good and the cracks removed by rebacking and restoring the canvas.

crayon

A stick of coloured chalk or wax used for drawing.

crazing

Fine cracks which appear on the glaze of pottery. These can be produced artificially for decorative purposes when they are known as **crackle glazes**.

credenza

A sideboard or cupboard.

crenellation

A parapet with alternating high and low sections. Also known as a BATTLEMENT.

crenelle

The peaked top of a helmet.
Also an **embrasure**.

crepidoma

The foundation of an ancient temple.

cresting moulding

A curved **moulding** projecting from the frame, like a cresting wave.

crevé

A hollow shape made by **aquafortis** for etching but rendered too wide. This is unacceptable for **intaglio** printing because any impression that is too hollow becomes dark grey.

Cristalleries de Saint-Louis
Together with **Baccarat**, the most important French fine coloured crystal glass. Although founded in 1767 the coloured glass for which it is most famous only began to be made from c1839.

crocket
In medieval architecture and in the decorative arts, the crocket is a painted ornamentation on the highest point of the building or on a piece of ornate furniture. A distinct biological meaning denotes the terminal branches on the horn of a stag, often depicted by painters in unnatural abundance.

cross hatching
Shading in **engraving** and **wood engraving** mainly to produce the effects of shadows. This is done by means of intersecting parallel lines, sometimes with centralised dots.

crypt
A vaulted chamber beneath the floors of a church.

C-scroll
Describes the shape of a scroll, often in combination with a reverse C-scroll. Part of the centre or corner ornament of a **rococo** frame. *Vide* **S-scroll**.

Cubism
An art movement of the early 20th century, following from **Post-Impressionism**, in which perspective was abandoned in favour of geometric shapes. The movement was a reaction against traditional methods and against impressionist concerns with light and colour. Leaders of the movement were Pablo Picasso (1881-1973) and George Braque (1882-1963), while Fernand Léger (1881-1955) and Juan Gris (1887-1927) were among the leading followers. In the beginning, colour and shapes were limited to a series of plains like an object viewed from differing perspectives. This became known as **analytical cubism**. This gradually evolved to become SYNTHETIC CUBISM when objects other than paint such as **collages** were applied to the painted image.

cuir bouilli
Literally, boiled leather. Known from early Saxon times, used in armoury, for making small boxes, small items of furniture, and in early bookbinding.

cuir-ciselé
A book cover decoration made by cutting the design in leather rather than by the more usual tooling.

culot
A small bunch of leaves, generally surrounding a stem. Derived from the French *culottes* (short trousers or knee breeches).

cupola
The rounded top of an edifice. A hemispherical roof over a circular building. Also a small tower built on a roof. From the Italian cupola (dome). Anything shaped like a cupola is called a **dome**.

curios

Vide **virtu**.

curlicue

An ornamental form or sculpture fantastically curled or twisted. Sometimes referred to as **rococo**.

cushion frame

Popular in the 18th century and revived in the 19th century, this modest frame has a flattish convex or rounded section, often ornamented with floral embellishment. These frames seldom exceeded 2½” across. Several variations have been identified, the most common being the so-called tulip pattern which has half-open buds stretching along a twisted rope pattern. *Vide* **Collins frame**.

cusped arch

A projecting point between small arcs in Gothic architecture. Thus, an arch whose inside edge is enriched by intersecting arcs.

cusped arch

cylex

Vide **kylix**.

cyma(tium)

A waved **moulding**. There are two kinds, CYMA RECTA, which is concave at the top and convex at the foot, and CYMA REVERSA which is convex at the top and concave at the bottom. Both shapes are referred to as **ogee**.

dabba

An instrument used for applying ink to a printing plate, usually in the preparation of **mezzotints** when it is preferred to a **roller**. An etcher's dabba traditionally consists of compressed cotton wool within a silk or leather sack.

Dadaism

An early 20th century movement, beginning in Zurich, concerned with all branches of art, which rejected all the customary artistic and social conventions, a natural reaction to the horrors of World War II. Although as a movement it survived only a short time, the negations led to a new form of imaginative art. The principle exponents were the German surrealist Max Ernst (1891-1976) who worked from Cologne, Kurt Schwitters (1887-1948), the French abstract sculptor Jean Arp (1887-1966), Marcel Duchamp (1887-1968), and the German satirist George Grosz (1893-1959).

dado

The **plinth** of a **column** or the cube of a **pedestal** between the base and the **cornice**.

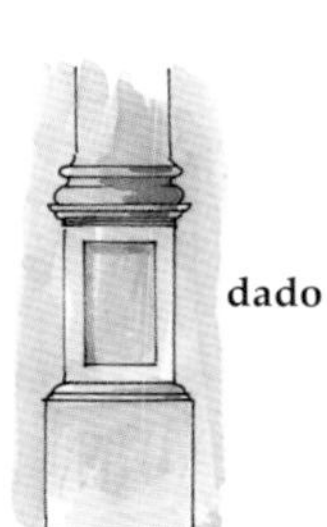

Daguerreotype

A procedure named after the French painter and photographer Louis-Jacques-Mandé Daguerre (1789-1851) who developed one of the first types of photograph using light to fix the image from a ***camera obscura*** in a mercury vapour and then upon an iodine sensitised silver plate.

damask

A word with several meanings. In the decorative arts it is used as a verb to embellish a metal with flowers or surface patterns, especially by the use of a different metal. Hence DAMASKEENING is the art of inlaying a metal upon the surface of another, also known as DAMASCENE WORK or DAMASKING. The skill involved is known as DAMASQUEENERY, from the French *damasquin* (to form something new). In textiles it refers to a type of weave.

dart
A dart or arrow shaped ornament.
Also a tapered tuck stitched in a garment.

date letter
A letter of the alphabet incised on to silver within a device to show the year of **assay**. In recent times this changes each year while, for most centres, the font used and the shape of the enclosing shield change every 25 years, the letter 'j' often excluded. Details vary according to the relevant assay office.

davenport
A compact lady's writing desk.

decadent(ce)
Literally, a falling away, a deterioration. When applied to individual activity, e.g. an artist or writer's 'decadent' work, it should refer to a diminution of creative power. When applied to a movement or a period or a civilisation, it acquires an increasingly subjective meaning, for what some may believe to be deterioration due to time may be interpreted by others as interesting variation. It is an epithet probably best avoided.

deckle
The rough, untrimmed edges of a sheet of hand-made paper, much used for watercolouring and for early books before the age of cloth binding. In modern books it is an affectation.

Deconstructivism
An architectural movement of the late 20th century which sought to break away from the shackles of conventional construction, creating buildings with unusual shapes and fragmented structures.

découpage
Paper cut into designs and fixed to a flat surface for decoration. Popular in Victorian times.

Degenerate Art
A term used by the Nazi government in Germany in the 1930s to describe western art of that time. In 1937 Munich held an exhibition of such works including examples by Paul Klee (1879-1940), Henri Matisse (1859-1954), and Pablo Picasso (1881-1973).

Delftware
A kind of glazed earthenware made in Delft. Characteristically blue and white. Much copied by Dutch and English manufacturers.

del(inevit)
Indicates the draughtsman of a print, usually appearing before the name.

della Robia ware
A kind of pottery used for works of art in relief, thought to have been first developed by the Italian sculptor Luca della Robbia (1400-1482). Vitreous glazes render the pottery impervious to damp and therefore suitable for external use e.g. as frescoes. The term is also sometimes used to describe a fine English terracotta used in architectural decoration from c1847.

demilune

Crescent shaped.

dentil

dentil

In architecture, a dentil is each individual rectangular block in a series decorating the underside of a **cornice**. Hence, as a framing term, it refers to a regularly spaced row of small blocks as part of a cornice. From the French *dentille* (a small tooth). In book binding a *DENTELLE* (from the French for lace) is a decorative border with a lacy pattern, usually in gilt, painted on the inner edges of the covers.

De Stijl

Dutch movement of art and design started in 1917 by Theo van Doesburg (1883-1931) which continued to formally exist until the early 1930s. The underlying idea was to bring to architecture and the arts consistent and ordered relations, 'a new plastic beauty of pure thought in which no image based on phenomena is involved but where numbers, measurements and abstract line have their place' [van Doesburg]. The best known painting disciple was Piet Mondrian (1872-1964). Also known as **Neo-plasticism**.

deux corps

A kind of furniture made in two parts, the upper section standing on a slightly wider top. The lower part usually comprises drawers, the upper part a cabinet.

dexter

The right-hand side. In heraldry it is the side of the shield fixed to the right arm, hence to the left of an observer. *cf* **sinister.**

diamante

Crystalline application to a fabric enhancing its glamour.

diaper

An ornamental design involving diamond shapes based on floral forms. When applied to frames the term refers to a repeated surface pattern of small diamond shapes filled with florettes or **quatrefoils**.

diarama

A scenic painting or paintings in which variations of illumination simulate different atmospheric effects. First devised in 1822 by Louis-Jacques-Mandé Daguerre (1789-1851), who introduced his second example in London's Regent's Park. A series of paintings is arranged in a darkened room so that a variety of effects can be introduced by varying the direction, intensity and colour of light, especially if the light is transmitted through the pictures which may be painted in thin colouring on two sides of the fabric such that changes, e.g. from day to night, can be made by changing the source of the illumination.

Die Brücke (The Bridge)

A group of artists founded in 1905, centred in Dresden. Early followers of **Expressionism**, the group sought to work from first principles, freely using strong colour, influenced by medieval German woodcuts and the strength of primitive African sculpture. Also influenced by the **Fauves**. Leading exponents were Ernst Kirchner (1880-1938), and Emile Nolde (1867-1955).

distemper
Paint made with glue or **size** instead of an oil base, used in house painting and also by artists seeking to cover large surfaces such as **murals** or **posters**.

distressed
Books or furniture and occasionally frames and paintings which show real or simulated signs of age and wear. The methods employed by those seeking to deceive are many and various.

Divisionism
Vide **Pointillism**.

divugavit
Vide **Exc(udit)**.

Dog of Fo
In Chinese decorative art, a dog-like creature, the guardian of Buddhist temples. Often replicated in furniture and porcelain.

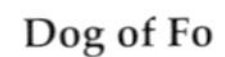

Dog of Fo

dome
Vide **cupola**.

Doric
The oldest and simplest of the three Greek orders of architecture. Generally regarded as the most subtle and delicate, both in refinement of outline and proportion. A Grecian Doric **column** has no base.

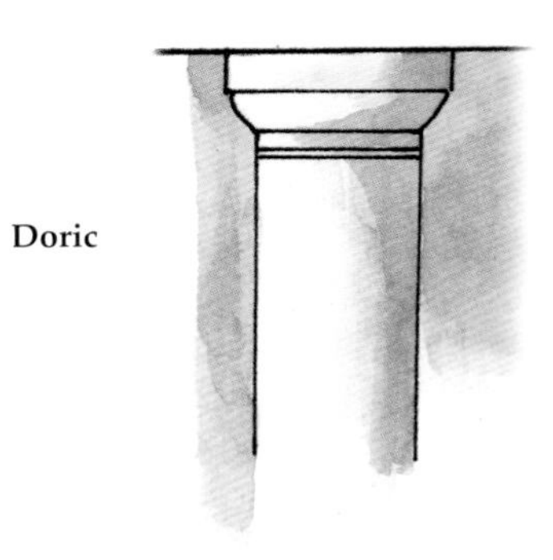

Doric

dotted prints
Vide ***manière criblée***.

dotting punch
A tool used for dotting directly on to an engraver's plate, mainly used for engraving maps.

double corner cupboard
Vide **buffet**.

double gilding
In water-gilding this is the process of adding a second layer of **gold leaf**.

Doucai
A Chinese vase of contrasting colours from the Yongzhong period (1723-1735) of the Qing dynasty. DOUCAI ENAMELLING, recently revived, was first developed by the Chinese in the 15th century.

drabware
Monochromatic neutral coloured style of **Wedgwood** earthenware.

dragon's blood
A dark red gum exuded from the fruit of some palms, the most common being the dragon tree, *Draceana draco*, a native palm of Malaya. Used as a glaze on porcelain figures and occasionally on frame **mouldings**.

drip
Vide **hood moulding**.

drypoint
A type of engraving, generally associated with etching, where the engraving tool is used on a bare copper plate without acid. Compared to line engraving when the tool is pushed across the plate, drypoint technique requires the needle to be drawn across. The method has been employed, on occasion, by many of the world's leading etchers including Albrecht Dürer (1491-1528), Harmensz van Rijn Rembrandt (1606-1669), David Wilkie (1785-1841), and Auguste Rodin (1840-1917).

dumb waiter
Vide **tier**.

dutch bath
One of three kinds of **mordants** used in etching. It is diluted hydrochloric acid mixed with chlorate of potash. Often used in conjunction with nitric acid.

dutch gold
Vide **brass**.

dutch leaf
Vide **brass**.

dutch metal
A kind of brass. A malleable alloy made up of eleven parts copper and two parts zinc used in leaf as a substitute for **gold leaf**. Also known as **dutch gold** or **schlag leaf**. It has a lacquer finish necessary to prevent tarnishing.

duty mark
The appearance of the Sovereign's head incised on silver indicating that duty has been paid. This first appeared in 1784 and continued until 1890. In Glasgow, the mark was not used until 1819 and in Dublin not before 1807.

Duveen frame
A style favoured by the art dealer Joseph Duveen (1869-1939), especially for his American clients. Based on period models but often excelling them in intricacy of detail and overall quality.

E

earthenware
A type of **ceramic** made from clay fired until it becomes porous when it is then glazed, rendering it impervious to liquids. The result is generally coarser and cheaper to make than other forms of ceramics which require greater heat and precision. Compared to **porcelain** it is opaque and differs also from **stoneware** by its porosity. It may be glazed or enamelled.

easel
A metal or wooden adjustable support for an artist's use when painting. Usually in the form of a collapsible tripod.

ébauche
In paintings and sculpture, outlines and edges are sometimes laid down in monochrome. This outline or preliminary sketch is the ébauche. Not to be confused with EBAUCHOIR, a chisel used by makers of statues.

ebonised
Stained and polished to simulate the appearance of **ebony**. Often associated with **ripple moulding**.

ebony
A name applied to various woods on account of their darkness and hardness. The best and most valuable is obtained from the tree *Diospyros ebenum*.

echinus
A rounded moulding below an **abacus** on a **Doric** or **Ionic capital**. On some **Sansovino frames**, the band is embellished with **egg-and-dart** or **flutes** interwoven with **volutes**.

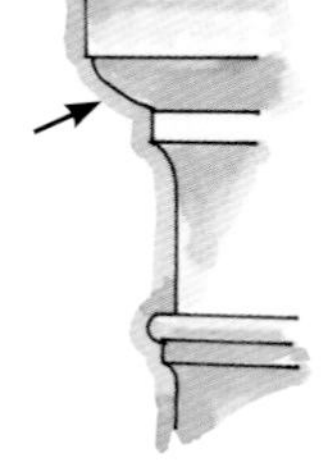
echinus

échoppe
A tool used in printmaking with a bevelled, oval point. The lines thus produced are known as SWELLING LINES.

écorché
The portrayal of a human or animal body with the skin removed. This is done to reveal musculature, exemplified in some of the horse engravings and paintings of the English painter George Stubbs (1724-1806).

effigy
The authentic representation of a person. Specifically applied to the sculpted figures on sepulchres and to the heads of state on coins and medals. In popular currency an effigy is not necessarily authentic.

egg-and-dart
A quarter-circle convexity carved with sheathed ovoids alternating with pointed forms producing an ornament shaped like an egg alternating with a dart. Also known as an EGG-AND-TONGUE and EGG-AND-ANCHOR. Commonly seen in **Kent frames**.

egg tempera
Paint with egg yolk, used for binding purposes.

Egyptian art
The architecture, painting and sculpture of more than 6,000 years ago, renowned for its refinement, scope and great beauty. The Sphinx of Ghizeh is the largest known sculpture in the world, in drawing, jewellery, glass, and wood carving the artists and craftsmen of Egypt were among the finest, but the height of their achievement were the great pyramids.

Eight Group
American realist painters who in 1907 organised a protest against certain policies of the National Academy of Design. They mounted an important and popular exhibition the following year which had a lasting influence on the course of modern American art.

electroplate
An article subjected to the electrolytic deposition of chromium or other metal to simulate silver.

electrotype
A printing technique to produce a copy by the electrolytic action of a copper deposit on a **mould**. This can produce such a good copy that to distinguish it from an Old Master print, for example, requires expert knowledge of the original. Also known as a **galvanotype**.

electuary
A small cabinet for holding medicines. In pharmaceutics it denotes a sweet powder for a patient to lick.

elutriation
The process of washing out and decanting as, for example, done sometimes by potters. Specifically, the separation of chemical constituents by suspension in a flow of gas or liquid.

embossing
To carve or mould in relief. A common method is by driving a blunt tool into wood to make the required pattern, then planing the surface down to the level of the sunken design before wetting it. According to the material being used an EMBOSSING-IRON or EMBOSSING-MACHINE or EMBOSSING-PRESS may be employed.

embrasure
The enlargement of the aperture of a door or window to provide more light or a wider vision.

embroidery
Decorative needlework applied in raised threads to linen and similar garments. Originally created by hand until the invention of an embroidery machine by M. Keilmann of Mulhause (France) in the mid 19th century.

E

emulsion
The dispersion of one liquid in another. In painting, EMULSION PAINT is paint which is made to form an emulsion with water.

enamel
In the painting of **miniatures**, enamel is a vitreous substance applied as a coating on metal or porcelain. More generally, enamel is any smooth, glossy surface other than glass.

encaustic paint
Pigments mixed with hot wax burned in as an **inlay**. A method popularised by the American pop artist, Jasper Johns (1930-).

encaustic tiles
Ornamental floorings and wall decorations widely used in churches and other large buildings in the 12th and 13th centuries, a practice revived in the 20th century.

encoignure
A small ornamental table or cabinet designed to fit into the corner of a room. A CORNER CUPBOARD differs by having no legs.

engaged frame
An early frame in which the panel of the painting fits into grooves. Common in the 16th century.

engobe
A coating of light-coloured earth mixed with water to give **earthenware** a smooth, easily cleaned surface.

engraving
Generally refers to a print produced by the use of a cutting instrument, e.g. a **burin**, on a metal, generally copper, or wood. There are two main types of engraving: **intaglio** and **relief**. Prior to photography engraving was the most common form of reproduction of an original work.

en plein air
In the open air, a phrase most commonly used in art in relation to the **Barbizon school** who frequently painted outdoors to portray natural light more accurately.

enrichment
A framing term describing a run of carved or moulded ornament.

entablature
On frames, this refers to the area below the **impediment** and above the **column** in a **tabernacle frame**, comprising the **architrave**, **cornice** and **frieze**. In architecture it is that part of a building immediately supported by **columns** and divided into the **architrave**, **cornice** and **frieze**.

entasis
The swelling or outward curve of the profile of the shaft of a **column**.

Environment(al) Art
Art, especially sculpture, of the late 20th century which sought to bring environmental issues to the forefront, either by its composition and/or the materials used in its production. It also refers to work intended for appreciation in the general (outdoor) environment.

ephemera
An item, generally a broadsheet or pamphlet, likely to be of interest for only a very short time, literally no more than a day, but in time perhaps becoming a collector's item as a result of its increasing rarity.

erotica
An image or book intended primarily to arouse sexual excitement. When sexual allusions are explicit it becomes **pornography**.

escarpa
Ornaments featuring **scrolls** and **volutes**, often on **Sansovino frames**.

escritoire
An elegant writing desk with drawers beneath.

escutcheon
A decorative motif used in furniture (indicating a shield or emblem) and in framing. It also describes the guard plate around a keyhole or handle. In heraldry it refers to the shield, the surface or 'field' of which is divided for descriptive purposes into eleven points or regions.

esquisse
The first preparatory sketch for a painting, an outline.

étagère
Vide **Whatnot**.

etching
A print made by applying corrosive acid on to a metal plate. Etchings may be 'hard ground', dating from the late 15th century, when the plate is hard, to resist the acid, or 'soft ground', popular in the late 18th and early 19th centuries, when the ground has a softer consistency made by the addition of grease such as tallow. There are distinctions between **engraving**, **line engraving** and **drypoint**, although these processes may be used two or three together on the same plate.

etching needle
Vide **needle**.

Etruscan
The art of ancient Etruria, located in central Italy. Although known for its large terracotta sculptures, it is best remembered for its **pottery**. There were four main types: (a) CANOPIC VASES, urns in the form of human heads, (b) BUCCHERO vases, black and unglazed, of ornamental design; (c) painted vases, in the Greek tradition; and (d) vases decorated in a glossy black varnish, with reliefs, called ETRUSCO-CAMPANIAN, made from the 3rd century B.C. ETRUSCAN WARE was a pottery made at Swansea in the mid 19th century, classically decorated in black or red.

étui
A small cylindrical case, often enamelled, for holding needles and similar objects.

exc(udit)
Indicates the publisher of a print. Synonyms include **divugavit**, **formis**.

E

Expressionism
A term applied to forms of art characterised by the expression of the emotions of the artist, however passionate or sombre. The impact of the Norwegian painter Edward Munch (1863-1944) was strong, as were a number of lesser known German artists among them Emil Nolde (1867-1956) and Ernst Kirchner (1880-1938). Also influenced were the **Die Brücke** and the **Der Blaureiter** groups, while in France followers included the Lithuanian born Chaim Soutin (1893-1943) and the Frenchman Georges Roualt (1871-1958). The emotions of the creators were given precedence over natural form, however grotesque the result.

'eye'
An expression used by art dealers and critics to denote a sensitive perception of quality or accurate attribution. A 'good eye' is a phrase used more often than its pejorative opposite.

F

facet
In jewellery this refers to any one side of a stone, especially a cut **gem**.

facsimile
An exact copy. A print or book may be copied in a variety of ways to appear as an original. In the 19th century engravings could be made from original drawings on paper causing consternation among some artists and collectors to this day as the distinction between an original and a copy (facsimile) is sometimes blurred.

faience
Decorated and glazed **porcelain**, a term loosely used leading to a variety of forms, thus FAIENCE FINE (pottery made from pipe-clay, often finished with a transparent glaze); *FAIENCE TRANSLUCIDE* (translucent earthenware, non-kaolinic porcelain); *FAIENCE D'ORION* (fine pottery from Orion in France). **Delftware** and **majolica** are among the best known examples of faience.

fake
A work having the false appearance of being genuine. A fake becomes a **forgery** by the application of a false signature or related documentation.

faldstool
A backless folding chair originally used by bishops; a small portable desk for kneeling at prayer.

false topaz
Vide **citrine**.

famille noire, rose, verte
Forms of Chinese porcelain from the 17th century onwards made primarily for export. The colour refers to the ground colour: noire (black), rose (red), or verte (green).

fan vault
A type of vault in which the supporting arches are fan-shaped, formed from cone-shaped CONOIDS.

fan vault

fascia
A **moulding** on a frame that appears in profile as a broad, shallow step. Classically, a long flat surface between mouldings on the **architrave** of a building.

fascicle
A portion of a book published separately. Also spelled FASCICULE. Loosely applied to any small bundle.

fashion
The popular taste or style. This can be a source of great misunderstanding as, for example, when critics or the media confuse what is fashionable with what is intrinsically meritorious or, by the same token, when perversely contrary views about current fashion are used to belittle merit. Fashion is manipulated by market forces and media attention. In the final analysis, the quality of changing artistic fashion is determined only by time.

faulting
The process of repair to small faults in the **moulding** of a frame where the **gilding** has not been properly fixed. This is usually done by resizing and regilding.

fauteuil
An opulent wooden chair with upholstered arms and open sides. Originally, a chair made in France for a presiding official, specifically for a member of the French Academy.

Fauve
An artist associated with the **Fauvist Movement**.

Fauvism
An art movement at its height based in Paris at the beginning of the 20th century, in which the treatment of colour is vividly expressionistic while not necessarily conforming to the colours of the natural world. Its principal proponents were Henri Matisse (1869-1954), André Dérain (1880-1954), Raoul Dufy (1877-1958) (who later developed his own separate style), and Maurice de Vlaminck (1876-1958).

fecit
Appearing after an artist's or craftsman's name indicating 'he made it', as for example, 'Stradivarius fecit'.

feldspar
A group of minerals extracted from rocks in the form of crystals used in the manufacture of **porcelain**. The most usual form is COMMON FELDSPAR, with a potash base. RESPLENDENT FELDSPAR is also known as **adularia** or **moonstone**. Feldspar is also known as FELSPAR.

fenestrate(d)
Having windows. Fenestration refers to the position and type of windows of a building. In architecture, it also refers to the design of windows.

festoon
Decorative chain or garland of foliage, flowers and/or fruit, often suspended in a curve between its two ends. A FESTOON-AND-TASSLE border is often seen in Roman and some later pottery. Also known as a **swag**.

fictile

Said of any material capable of being moulded into shape. Thus in pottery a FICTILE MOSAIC, an ancient Roman type, is one in which the **tesserae** are made of an artificial vitreous compound enabling it to change form.

figurative

A painting or sculpture in which the human figure, or figures, predominate.

filigree

Ornamental work of fine gold, silver or copper wire formed into delicate tracery work. An ancient craft of jewellers, more recently a speciality of northern Italy.

fillet

A narrow flat step between two **mouldings** in a frame. Also a small band between the **volutes** of a **column**. In carpentry it refers to an added triangular piece of wood to round off an interior angle. It is also a tool, sometimes called a FILLET-CUTTER having a revolving wheel with one or more raised bands on its circumference used by bookbinders for impressing a line or parallel lines on the covers. A FRENCH FILLET is a triple fillet producing unevenly spaced lines in gold. In heraldry, a fillet can be either a bearing in the lower position corresponding to the lower edge of the chief, or a bearing comprising a quarter of the **bordure**.

fin de siècle

Used to attribute anything that shows characteristics commonly associated with the end of the 19th century, the time when the old order was said to be changing, heralding emancipation from the traditional aesthetic and moral order.

fine art

Arts purporting to have an aesthetic character, especially architecture, the **graphic arts** and **sculpture**.

fine clay

Vide **clay**.

finial

A turned ornament finishing off the apex of a roof, the cover of a piece of silverware, or the top of a grandfather clock. Generally less ornate than a **crocket**.

fl. (floruit)

Used after an artist's name to indicate the recorded dates during which he flourished. Generally used only when precise dates of birth and death are unknown or unclear.

flambé

From the French to singe. Ascribed to **porcelain** which, because of very high furnace temperature and the use of copper oxide, has an irridescent red lustre.

flat

In frames, a wide flat area, often adjoining the picture. It is also loosely used to describe the appearance of an oil painting with too little varnish or none at all.

Most often applied to figures and vases. Originally known in China five centuries ago, the technique was first developed in Europe by the Royal Doulton factory at the beginning of the 20th century. Not to be confused with the two meanings of FLAMBEAU, (a) a large, ornate candlestick, usually made of bronze, and (b) the symbol of life.

flèche

A tall thin spire, usually without an underlying tower. Frequently seen on French Gothic churches.

fleuron

fleuron

A flower-shaped decoration or ornament.

flock prints

A rare type of print similar to a **woodcut** except that the impressions are made in paste rather than in ink. This renders the print softer with a rich texture, reminiscent of a textile.

Florentine fresco

A kind of open air (fresco) or wall painting. when the **ground** is covered in lime kept moist during the application of paint. First practised in Florence.

Florentine mosaic

Mosaic made with precious or semi-precious stones inlaid in a surface of black marble or similar material. Although generally smooth the design can sometimes be in **high relief**. Usually applied to the tops of small objects.

fluting

Often seen in **neo-classical** frames, fluting refers to a series of parallel concave grooves, often cut across the **hollow** of a frame at right-angles to the side. As a verb it refers to the making of a groove or furrow the result of which is a FLUTE.

Fluxos

An international network of artists, composers and writers who sought to introduce chance into their creations. Attitude is given more significance than method or style. Although anarchic and anti-art it carried social connotations. The Lithuanian artist George Macuinas (1931-1978) organised the first Fluxos Art event in New York in 1961. Derived from the French word *fluer*, to flow.

flying buttress

flying buttress

Vide **buttress**.

foil embossed

A procedure whereby prints are made on heavy paper, using a metallic foil before being stamped on to a surface leaving the embossed area with a fine metallic finish.

folly
A useless, whimsical ornamental building, often of classical style in the form of a tower.

font
The kind or size of typeface. These are becoming increasingly varied with the development of modern typography. Unfortunately, too few books nowadays inform the reader of the font used.

fontana maiolica
Vide **maiolica**.

forgery
A work becomes a forgery when a false signature is applied. Although generally the signature is on the work itself, it may also be applied to related documentation. *Vide* **fake**, **pastiche**.

form
A difficult word with many meanings. At its simplest it refers to the shape, colour or arrangement of an artistic work. It can also mean the essential characteristic of an object. Plato, for example, distinguished between three forms of an object as distinct from a concept, the perfect form, made by God, an object made by man, and a copy as produced by a painter. In the realm of aesthetics greater complexity has been introduced with the notion of **significant form** by art critics such as Clive Bell and Roger Fry.

format
The shape and size of a book. More specifically, the number of folds in the original printed sheet forming its constituent leaves. The principle formats are FOLIO (2°), QUARTO (4°), OCTAVO (8°) and DUODECIMO (12°). The SHEET is the printer's unit, the LEAF the bibliographer's, and the GATHERING is the binder's.

formis
Vide **Exc(udit)**

foul-biting
In making an **etching** the **mordant** can seep under the wax ground accidentally. It can also be done deliberately, the surface being roughened by a feather or fine brush when it is known as a **brush etching**.

found object *(objet trouvé)*
A curiosity or freak of nature resembling an animal or human form which **Surrealists** in particular employed to animate their fantasies. Also used by artists such as the English war artist Paul Nash (1889-1946) to introduce a sense of mystery.

foxed (-ing)
Brownish-yellow spots, first noted in 1848, which appear on paper due to chemical action if the paper has been improperly bleached during its manufacture, known as fox marks. Usually caused by damp or unventilated conditions and accentuated by impurities in the paper. Of particular significance for pencil drawings, prints, books and watercolours, although on drawings minor foxing can generally be removed.

frame(s)
The structure that secures a picture in place. The five main types of frame are: **Cassetta**, **Reverse**, **Sansovino**,

Tabernacle and **Tondo**. For these and many sub-types see under their main name.

fresco

A kind of watercolour painting in which the paint is applied to wet, freshly prepared plaster allowing the colours to penetrate and become fixed. Mainly used during the Renaissance for wall paintings. Although best suited to warmer climes, it has been tried in northern Europe and most recently revived in Mexico and North America. *Vide* **Florentine fresco**.

F

fret

As a noun, a fret is an interlaced or ornamental work common in Grecian art and architecture. As a verb it is to introduce or create a fret. In heraldry it is a **charge** interlaced with a **lozenge**.

frieze

The central flat area between the inner and outer mouldings of a frame. Also refers to a band of architectural decoration, especially along a wall near the ceiling.

frieze

frottage

A painting technique developed by the German artist Max Ernst (1891-1976) which involves rubbing the grain or pattern of an uneven surface such as leaves or wood grain across a sheet of paper over which a pencil is passed. The textured results can then be used in making a **collage**.

fugitive colour

Paint whose durability cannot be relied upon. Examples are carmine, mauve, geranium lake and, among watercolours, chrome brown, chrome yellow, rose Carthane and Vandyke brown.

fustian

A strong twilled cotton cloth with a short nap.

Futurism

An art movement which also encompassed literature and music, founded by the Italian poet Filippo Tomasso Marienetti (1876-1944). This was a conscious response, with its own manifesto, to the gathering mechanical and technological developments of the 20th century. It was the first attempt to unify attitude and tempo in the arts. The movement sought to remove itself from all past influences. Adherents among painters included the Italian Umberto Baccioni (1882-1916) and another Italian, Carlo Carrà (1881-1966), who subsequently joined Giorgio de Chirico (1888-1978) in an imaginative style they christened **metaphysical**. A separate development was introduced by the Russian painter and philosopher Pavel Filonov (1883-1941) who christened his intense multifaceted work **Analytical Art** or **Universal Flowering**. Although Futurism did not survive the first world war its influence continued long after, especially in Russia.

G

G

gable

The upper part of a wall at the end of a ridged roof. By extension, the end wall of a house or a triangular canopy above a doorway or window. Small examples are known as GABLETS.

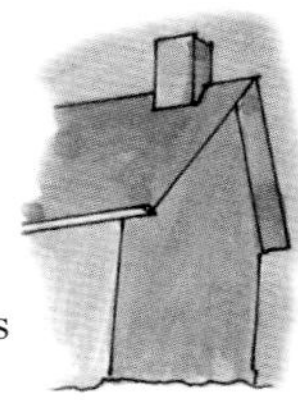

gable

gable-boards

Vide **bargeboard**.

gadrooning

Decoration, especially on furniture, frames and silverware, comprising a run of continuous curves in a series forming an ornamental edge. Also known as **knurling** or **nulling**.

Gallé

A type of glassware developed by the French designer Émil Gallé (1846-1904). Together with René **Lalique** his designs helped define the **Art Noveau Movement**. Although Gallé glass continued to be made until 1926, its finest work was over by 1921. Wares made between 1904 and 1921 are signed and preceded by a star. The best work is characterised by the use of opaque glass, often of irregular shape, carved or etched with natural motifs, especially plants.

gallet(ing)

To introduce fragments of stone into coarse masonry while the mortar is still wet.

galuchet

Vide **shagreen**.

garde-de-vin

Vide **cellarette**.

gargoyle

A spout usually in the form of a grotesque human or animal head, projecting from a gutter to drain water therefrom. Architectural humour.

garniture

Decorated accessories or adornments as, for example, the side ornaments of an ornate French mantel clock.

gem(stones)

Any **precious** or **semi-precious stone**.

genre

In its general sense it refers to any specific kind of style. More specifically, genre painting describes compositions from everyday life, particularly domestic scenes. The most famous genre painters were working in the 17th century in the Low Countries, especially Jan Vermeer (1632-1675) and Pieter de Hooch (c1629-c1684).

geode
A stone or pebble, usually of quartz, with an interior cavity the walls of which may be lined with crystals. Collected for their beauty.

G

Georgian
Styles, especially of architecture and silver, prevalent during the reign of the four Georgian kings (1714-1830).

German Silver
Vide **paktong**.

gesso
A compound of chalk or plaster and glue, used to prepare a surface for painting or **gilding**. Italian word for **gypsum**, although in Italy calcium sulphate is used but elsewhere calcium carbonate.

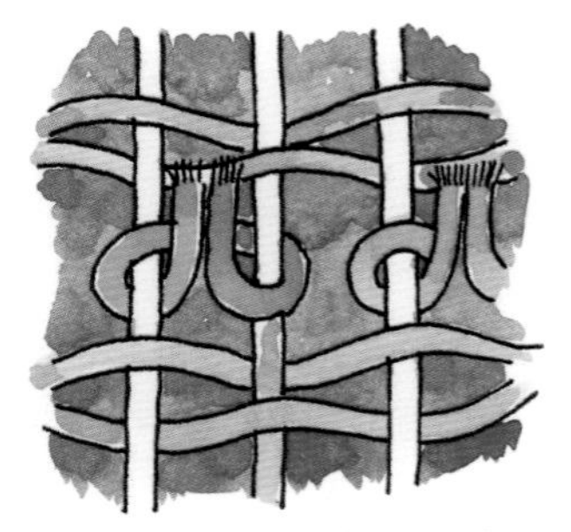

Ghiordes knot

Ghiordes knot
With the **Senneh knot** it is one of the two most common forms of knotting in the weaving of Oriental rugs and carpets. Traditionally used in Turkey and the Near East. It is made by looping a knot round two warp-threads and bringing the ends of yarn, forming the **pile**, out between them.

giclée
From the French 'to spray'. A modern printing process producing good colour accuracy. Print images are made from high resolution digital scans using best quality ink.

gilding
The application of **gold leaf** to a surface. This may be done chemically by electroplating with gold or manually by laying gold leaf on to an adhesive surface. Synthetic materials to simulate gold leaf are sometimes used. A GILDER is one who gilds. A GILDING-WAX is made from beeswax with red ochre, alum, borax or vitriol, and is occasionally used to advance the colour. A GILDING-TOOL is a handled brass hand-stamp used by bookbinders. A GILDER'S CUSHION is a flat padded surface with a raised collar surrounding one end to protect the gold leaf during gilding. A GILDER'S TIP is a broad fine brush used for collecting loose gold leaf from the surface of an article after gilding has been completed.

girandole
A branched candlestick, either free standing or attached with a bracket to a wall;

or an earring with a central precious stone surrounded by smaller ones.

Glasgow Boys

A loose association of Scottish artists based primarily in Glasgow, working during the last 20 years of the 19th century. They were Sir D Y Cameron (1865-1945), James Elder Christie (1847-1914), Joseph Crawhall (1861-1913), T Millie Dow (1848-1919), David Gauld (1865-1936), Sir James Guthrie (1859-1930), J Whitelaw Hamilton (1860-1932), George Henry (1858-1943), E A Hornel (1864-1933), William Kennedy (1859-1918), Sir John Lavery (1856-1941), J Pittendrigh Macgillivray (1856-1938), Harrington Mann (1864-1937), Arthur Melville (1855-1904), T Corson Morton (1859-1928), Stuart Park (1862-1933), James Paterson (1854-1932), Sir George Pirie (1864-1946), Alexander Roche (1861-1921), R Macaulay Stevenson (1854-1952), Grosvenor Thomas (1855-1923), and Edward A Walton (1860-1922). Not to be confused with the GLASGOW FOUR (Charles Rennie Mackintosh & associates), or the GLASGOW GROUP (1957 onwards), or the GLASGOW GIRLS (1880-1920).

glass

Material made by the fusion of silica with a variety of bases. It is usually brittle, durable, hard and transparent. There are many types according to preparation and usage. Its principal art form is **stained glass**.

glass mosaic

Vide **mosaic**.

glass prints

In the 18th century a print, usually a **mezzotint**, was cemented with a water-resistant fixative on to a piece of glass, the paper was then moistened before removal, leaving ink outlines which were then painted from the reverse. From the 19th century the paper was exposed under a glass plate whereupon, because of the effect of light on light-sensitive paper, it reacted as a photographic negative.

G

glazing

The glass which protects a painting, watercolour or print. Thus a work said to be 'glazed' indicates that it is behind protective glass. Glaze can also refer to a thin coat of transparent paint used to modify the colour beneath. In ceramics a vitreous substance is used, usually a special kind of glass.

Gluck frame

A two or three-stepped frame, generally white, which the artist Gluck (Hannah Gluckstein, 1895-1975) patented in 1933, following her exhibition at the Fine Art Society in London.

glyphs

Vide **triglyphs**.

Gobelin(s)

Fine French tapestry and upholstery, founded 1450 by a family of that name and nationalised by the French government in the mid 17th century. Hence GOBELIN STITCH, and GOBELINS, tapestry made at the Paris factory.

gold

A precious shiny metal giving its name to a yellow colour. Used extensively in picture framing.

gold leaf

Gold beaten into a very thin sheet. An ounce of gold can be beaten to cover an area of more than 200 square feet. Gold is rolled into a ribbon then cut into small pieces before being beaten repeatedly against gold beaters. GOLD BEATERS' MOULD comprises several hundred leaves of parchment, vellum, and gold beaters' skin, fixed to a metal mould between which flattened pieces of gold are placed and then hammered until the required thinness of leaf is obtained. GOLD BEATERS' SKIN is made from the outer membrane of the large intestine of an ox. *Vide* **gilding**.

gold size

The adhesive compound used to fix **gold leaf** in place. In oil gilding it is oil-based, in water gilding it is water-based. The water-based gold size is a combination of clay and size. *Vide* **bole**. It can also refer to a mixture of **chrome yellow** and **varnish** for use in gold printing.

goldstone

Vide **schmelze**.

Gothic

Generally, an architectural style which originated in France in the mid 12th century, succeeding the Romanesque period and lasting until the 16th century. More loosely, it refers to any art form reminiscent of the Middle Ages. GOTHIC REVIVAL refers to the revival of this style which occurred between the late 18th and early 19th centuries. In printing it refers to old fashioned German or **sanserif** (i.e. without any projection in the stroke of a letter).

gouache

A painting **medium** using opaque pigments ground in water and then thickened with a glue. Gouache can refer both to the medium itself and to a painting in which the medium has been used.

gouge

A printmaker's chisel for scooping out parts of the plate to be erased, most often used for heraldic engraving. A form of **scooper** (scorper). *Vide* **tint tool**.

graffiti

Words or images, drawn, scribbled or sprayed on a wall or poster. The singular is graffito, thus GRAFFITO DECORATION is the covering of a unicolour surface with paint or other material in a different colour and then scratching through the outer layer of paint to reveal the colour beneath.

graphic arts

All forms of art which have a visual hand worked nature. Generally taken to encompass calligraphy as well as design, drawing, painting and printing.

graver

Vide **burin**.

griffin
A mythological creature having the body and legs of a lion and the head and wings of an eagle, symbolising agility and strength. Also an emblem of vigilance.

grisaille
A type of painting in grey monochrome; sometimes used in the designing of stained glass windows.

groined vault
An arch supporting a roof whereby the curved intersections cross each other at an angle.

grotesque
Intricate anthromorphic and/or zoomorphic surface ornament. Said to be derived from the painted decoration in Nero's Golden House. Based upon Renaissance **arabesques** with human figures terminating in animal or imaginative floral forms. In recent times it has come to be applied mainly to rude, ugly or deformed human forms.

ground
A metal plate, usually copper, used for **etching** and **engraving**. Preparing (laying) the ground is done in various ways. The earliest and most common method was for powdered **resin** to be placed in a box before being blown in to a cloud; the plate was then placed in the box, and all openings closed, so that the dust settled evenly on the plate before becoming fixed to the plate by heat. Alternatively, the dust could be shaken from a muslin bag. Another method was to dissolve the resin in wine so that when spread evenly the wine slowly dissolves leaving a dry ground. Similarly, in the case of paintings, the ground refers to the preparatory material laid on the canvas or other material before oil paint is introduced.

Group of Seven
A group of Canadian landscape painters, formally recognised in 1920. Their style was colourful and expressionistic. The first major movement in Canadian art.

Guanyin
The Chinese goddess of mercy, often depicted in statuary and in paintings.

gueridon
Vide **torchère**.

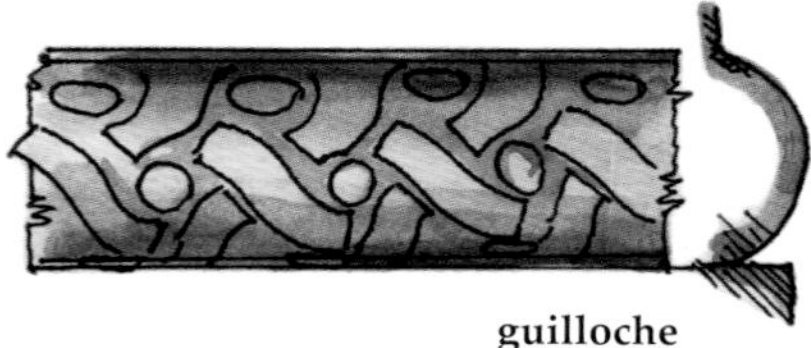

guilloche

guilloche
A kind of frame decoration comprising a run of stylised beaded ribbons, forming a series of circles, sometimes enclosed within a rosette. Seen also in architecture and metalwork.

gutta
A drop. Specifically, a technical term for a block-shaped ornament supporting the series of tablets usually with three vertical grooves in a **Doric frieze**.

Not to be confused with GUTTA-PERCHA, a gum used in, among other things, 19th century book binding and golf balls.

gypsum
Hydrous sulphate of calcium, usually white. The fine grained white or delicately coloured form is known as **alabaster**, used for ornamental purposes.
Vide **gesso**.

G

H

Hague School
Dutch painters centred in and around The Hague, working 1860-1900. Mostly landscapes but also interiors, with a sombre palette. The most influential members were Bernard Blommers (1845-1914), Jozef Israels (1824-1911), Jacob Maris (1837-1889), Matthijs Maris (1839-1917), Anton Mauve (1838-1888), and Taco Mesdag (1829-1902).

half bound (or half calf)
A book with the spine and corners bound in leather or vellum, the rest being in cloth.

half tone print(ing)
A reproduction printed from a photographically produced block in which differing tones of grey result from light being reflected from a photographic image through a closely meshed screen which produced a series of dots. Variations in screen size determined the proximity of the dots and therefore the intensity of light.

hallmark
Named after the Goldsmiths' Hall in London, it is the official stamp or group of stamps on silver and gold as proof of genuineness.

hamatan
A fine quality goat skin leather used in luxury bookbinding.

hammerbeam

hammerbeam
A short beam projecting from a wall attached to a roof rafter, usually found in pairs. Commonly supported by a rib resting on a **corbel**. Rarely, an entire roof is supported by hammerbeams, one of only two remaining in England is the restored barn at Westenhanger Castle in Kent.

hanging buttress
Vide **buttress**.

harmony
In a work of art the pleasing effect produced by the agreement, connection, similarity and unity of colour, form and light. This usually implies the absence of jagged or jarring edges or notes.

harpy
A mythical beast having the body of a woman and the wings and claws of an eagle. Originally, the harpies were the name given to storm winds in Grecian mythology, depicted in early art as winged women, usually two or three.

hatching
Shading on a drawing, map or print made by the introduction of close parallel lines. When these lines cross it is CROSS-HATCHING.

hatchment
The full armorial bearings of a deceased person. Usually fixed in a church memorial or on a tombstone.

hazzling
Zig-zag **chasing** in **gesso** for enriching flat areas of carving in the late 17th and early 18th centuries. Hence, to make such chasing is to HAZZLE.

helix
A spiral ornament.

Hepplewhite
Style of furniture developed by the English designer George Hepplewhite (1720-1786). Characterised by lightness, elegance and grace.

heraldry
The art and science of bearing arms, signifying genealogy and social precedence.

Herbert frame
Style developed by the English artist, precursor to the Pre-Raphaelites, John Rogers Herbert (1810-1890), in the mid 19th century. In **low relief**, of modest size, and with only minimal bold ornament.

herm
Architectural term derived from the Greek god Hermes: a squared pillar surmounted with a stylised head. Also a head cast in a frame **moulding**.

highlight
The brightest small part of a drawing or painting. Used more loosely to indicate that part of the pictorial image to which the artist/designer wished to direct attention.

high relief
When a **carving** or **moulding** stands out from the surface. *Vide* **low relief**.

High Renaissance
Vide **Renaissance**.

hockey
A little-used term to describe a modern frame having a plain flat cushion top, like a hockey stick.

hollow
A term in framing to denote a concave section, often the main curve of a frame.

hood mould
The projecting part of an arch over a door or window, common in medieval times. Also called a **drip**, **label** or **weather-moulding**.

hue
Vide **colour**.

humanism
In terms of art, humanism refers to an attitude of mind that turns toward the human rather than the divine. A driving force behind the **Renaissance**, when art concentrated more on rational enquiry than religious dogma.

husk
In framing, a line of short, flat leaves, occasionally in single form.

hyaline
Glasslike; from the Greek *hualos* (glass).

Hydra
A classical monster, a dragon with seven heads which grew again after being decapitated by Hercules.

Hyperrealism
An art movement of the early 21st century, the natural successor to **Photorealism**. Essentially photographic, the aim was to portray the essence of a subject more subtly and comprehensively than can be achieved photographically.

I

icon(ography)
An image, usually representative of a figure of high prestige or a high ideal. Thus ICONOGRAPHY is the study of images, especially portraits. ICONOCLASM is the breaking of images, as practised in Cromwellian times; hence more loosely applied to an attack on any hallowed belief or tradition. Not to be confused with ICHNOGRAPH(Y), a map or ground plan of a building, nor with ICONOLOGY, a critique of the meaning in a work, nor with ICONOSTASIS, an icon-bearing screen in an Eastern Church.

ilfrachrome
Vide **cibachrome**.

illuminated
In the art of book illustration, manuscripts of the Middle Ages contained intricate drawings in rich bodycolour and gold. Such works are said to be illuminated and those who executed them ILLUMINATORS.

image
The visual representation of the subject of a painting or sculpture. When considering size, the image is distinguished from the overall size which includes the frame.

Imari
Japanese **porcelain** from the town of Arita. Characteristically, a blue colour on a white background, often depicting flora.

imbrication
A pattern of overlapping decorations, usually scales or leaves resembling roofing tiles.

imp.
Appearing on a print, meaning 'he/she printed it'; from the Latin *impressit*.

impasto
The thickness of paint on a painting. When thick it defines a method of oil painting whereby opaque paint is heavily laid on, generally with a **palette knife**, sometimes so thickly as to give a three-dimensional effect.

impost
The upper part of a **pillar** carrying an **arch**. On a **Sansovino frame** it comes between the **abacus** and the **archivolt**. Away from the world of art, an impost is any form of taxation.

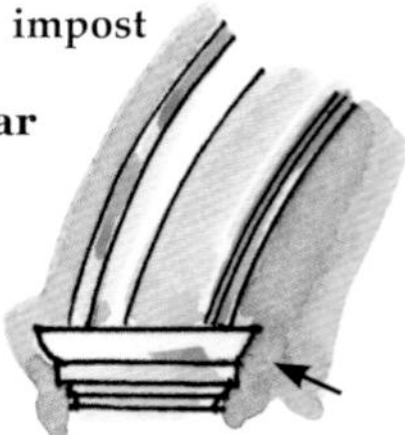

impression

In printing, an image taken from a block, plate or stone. The first impression refers not to the first copy produced but to the number of copies taken from the original plate. Impression may also refer to the quality of printing.

Impressionism

A French artistic movement, originating in the Paris Exhibitions 1874-76, aimed at portraying the beauties of transient light by means of colour, especially in landscapes. This predisposition, led by Claude Monet (1846-1926) and Camille Pissarro (1831-1903), underwent continuous development. Heavily involved were Auguste Renoir (1841-1919), Paul Cézanne (1881-1906), Paul Gauguin (1848-1903), Georges Seurat (1859-1891), and Vincent van Gogh (1853-1890); also Edgar Degas (1834-1917) although he was more interested in **figurative painting**, especially ballet dancers and horses. In due course, evolving from Impressionism, **Modern Art** took off. The name Impressionism arose from the title of a work by Monet *Impressions: soleil vivant* (1874).
Vide **Neo-impressionism, pointillism**

incidit

Vide **sculp**.

incunabula

Books printed before 1501. In recent years the word has been given the wider meaning of anything originating from the earliest stages of that thing.

India paper

A misleading abbreviation for INDIA PROOF PAPER, the same as CHINA PAPER, used for proofs of **engravings** and sometimes for **lithographs** and **woodcuts**. Made from bamboo fibre, it is absorbent, soft, and very thin. Also OXFORD INDIA PAPER, an opaque paper used in printing, first made by the Oxford University Press in 1875.

Indian carpet

Vide **Oriental carpets**.

inlay

The introduction of material, generally wood, into the body of another surface, common in furniture design between 1550 and 1650. Not to be confused with **marquetry**, introduced c1680, nor with **parquetry**.

installation art

Art designed for a specific indoor space. It may consist of lights or material objects. In most cases the use of the term 'art' (rather than e.g. design) becomes questionable.

intaglio

One of two classes of **engraving**, the other being **relief**. A process of printing from an engraved design. *Intaglio* is the Italian for engraving. In intaglio printing the lines represent the design itself. INTAGLIOTYPE is a design process using intaglio on a metal plate coated with zinc oxide before being smoothed hydraulically.

intarsia

The craft of using wood **inlays**, first developed in 15th century Italy.

integral

An early 16th century frame in which the frame and the **panel** are made from the same piece of wood. Attractive when used for early portraits.

inven(it)

Indicates the designer, generally preceding the name. The same as **composuit**.

I

Ionic

Relating to the Ionian islands. One of the three Greek orders of architecture distinguished by the scroll shaped **volutes** on either side of the **capital**. The Ionic school of painting prospered in the second half of the 5th and early 6th centuries B.C.

Ionic

Iranian carpet

Vide **Oriental carpets**.

Italian Primitives

An important group of Italian painters of the **Byzantine** and **Early Renaissance** periods. There were two main centres: Sienna and Florence. In Sienna the major exponents were Lippio Memmi (c1291-1356), Pietro Lorenzetti (1290-1348) and Sano di Pietro (1406-1481). In Florence they were Giotto (c1267-1337), Fra Angelico (c1395-1455), Lorenzo Monaco (c1370-1425), Masaccio (1401-1428), and Filippo Lippi (1406-1469).

ivorine

Cellulose nitrate. A translucent white plastic sheet used by miniaturists as a substitute for **ivory**. Since 1994 made in Italy. Also known as **xylonite**. Cooler to the touch than ivory, with a slight smell of camphor used in its production.

ivory

Hard creamy substance obtained from the tusks of various animals. Artificial substitutes are now generally replacing the use of organic originals.

J

Jacobean
Work performed in, or designs characteristic of, the reigns of James I and II (1603-1688). *Vide* **Jacobin**, **Jacobite**.

Jacobin
Refers to the period when the French revolutionaries of this name were active, 1788-1799.

Jacobite
Work performed, or characteristic of the period, when the Stuarts sought to regain the English throne 1689-1746.

jade
A tough usually green stone used since pre-historic times, particularly by oriental carvers, for making utensils, ornamental decorations and figures. Spinach jade, so-called because of its colour, is especially desirable. A smooth rather than a jagged carving is to be preferred. Also refers to the colour itself.

jamb
The weight-bearing side of a door, fireplace, or window.

Japan
In art the term has two distinct meanings. (1) A liquid originating in Japan, made by cooking gum **shellac** with **linseed** oil to produce a kind of **varnish**; also JAPAN LACQUER produced by cooking asphaltum with linseed oil thinned with turpentine. (2) Old Japan, or **Imari**, a **porcelain** having a white ground and decorated with dark blue under the glaze, and other coloured enamels.

japanning
Using a hard, generally black glossy asphaltum **varnish**. Originally from Japan and used on furniture and as a finish, occasionally applied to picture frames.

jardinière
An ornamental open container or table for holding flowers. When in cabinet form is usually lined with lead.

jasper
A kind of opaque quartz. JASPER WARE is a form of white or powder-blue stoneware first developed by Josiah **Wedgwood** (1730-1795).

jesse(s)

In falconry, the strap(s) for hawks' bells. Sometimes called a JESS.

Jesuit cable

Vide **baroque**.

Jesuit style

Vide **baroque**.

jet

Fossilised coal.

jubilee mark

J

A mark on silver bearing the heads of George V and Queen Mary commemorating the 25th year of their reign. Found on silver plate 1933-1935.

Jugendstil

Vide **Art Nouveau**.

K

Kakiemon
Superb Japanese enamelled porcelain from Arita, first made in the mid 17th century. Declared a national treasure by the Japanese Government in 1971.

kaolinite clay
Vide **clay**.

keep
A tower. The strongest edifice of a medieval castle.

Kelim
Vide **Oriental carpets**.

Kent
An 18th century **box** frame with projecting square corners, a flat **frieze** embellished with sand or patterned ornament, and a raised outer edge carved with **egg-and-dart** or similar architectural ornament. Named after the English architect and landscape gardener, William Kent (c1685-1745).

key
A taper-shaped piece of wood used to secure a **mitre joint**, or to tighten a wooden frame by insertion at its corners; also known because of its shape as a FEATHER KEY. A **butterfly key** is a variant.

keystone
Vide **voissoir**.

kitsch
Defined in the *Oxford English Dictionary* as 'garish, pretentious, or sentimental art, especially as appreciated in a perverse or self-conscious way'.

knull
A technical term used in framing to describe the top surface of a **moulding**.

knurling
Vide **gadrooning**.

kodansu
Japanese chest, usually with three drawers. It is a small form of **tansu**, a Japanese chest of furniture.

koro
Japanese word for an incense burner.

kovshi

Russian drinking vessel in the shape of a boat with a single extended curved handle. The best examples are elaborately enamelled.

Kutani

A style of early Japanese porcelain characterised by the use of multiple colours and strong designs. Originated in 1655 in the village of Kutani ('nine valleys'). Early wares, known as KO-KUTANI, are now extremely rare, having been in production for only 60 years.
In c1800 the style enjoyed a revival with the products, KUTANI-SHOGA, geared primarily for export.

kylix

An elegant shallow vase or drinking cup used in early Greek antiquity; also spelled CYLIX. Not to be confused with a KYLE, a primitive type of American lamp.

kyrin

Mythical Chinese creature with a lowslung, long body, cloven feet and often horns. Known also in Japanese and Korean mythology.

L

label
Vide **hood mould**.

lac
In parts of S.E. Asia, the female of the lac insect, *carteria lacca*, exudes a substance on to the twigs of certain trees. This is then collected and known as STICK-LAC. SEED-LAC, used in the making of **shellac**, is obtained by removing the resinous accretion and treating it in water. LAC-LAKE is used in the preparation of carmine coloured paint.

lace
When applied to ornamental traceries of thread it takes many designs and forms according to the purpose for which it is made and the place from whence it originated.

lacquer
The original Oriental process involved an opaque varnish derived in part from the **lac insect**, made from **shellac**, dissolved in alcohol with coloured and other materials added, or from the gum of the Chinese tree *Rhus vernicifera*. Its precise composition varied according to the place where made and the intended purpose. Also refers to a varnished decoration with the appearance of polished enamel.

laid down
A print that has been pasted upon paper; avoided by purists.

Lalique
A type of solid but elegant glassware first developed by the French designer René Lalique (1860-1945) including domestic ornaments, jewellery, clocks and automobile hood forms. With Émil **Gallé**, his work epitomised and helped define the **Art Deco** and **Art Nouveau** Movements. Lalique glass is still made.

lambrequin
A French term for short pieces of wooden ornament imitating textile fringes. In the decorative arts it describes an object resembling a lambrequin, as in some Chinese porcelain, in which an upper part of the item has unbroken decoration while the lower part has a jagged or ornamental outline.

landscape shape

A painting or frame in which the width is greater than its height. This contrasts with **portrait shape** where the height is greater than the width.

lapjoint

In framing, a corner joint with the wood on one side overlapping the adjoining side.

lappet

A small flap in a **moulding** usually adjacent to the edge.

lattice window

Vide **mousharaby**.

laurel leaf

As the name implies, the depiction of a laurel leaf, sometimes with berries, used to decorate the **top edge** of a frame. Also seen in some silverware.

Lawrence frame

A frame of **ogee** section with a small-scale running generalised foliage and scroll pattern, often with shell or foliage corners. Named after the English portrait painter Sir Thomas Lawrence (1769-1830), this being his favourite style. Straight-sided and heavy.

leaf-and-berry

A type of twisted leaf frame most common in the late 17th century, with embellishments of berries and leaves.

leaf-and-tongue

A running pattern, often applied to the back or **sight edge** of a frame, with leaves and tongues alternating.

leaf-and-tongue

lectern

A reading desk in a church or lecture theatre.

Lely frame

A term sometimes used to describe a **panel frame**, named after the anglicised Dutch artist Sir Peter Lely (1618-1680), although in fact the type only became popular after the artist's death.

lesene

Thin vertical strips of stone or simulated stone decorating the facade of a medieval building. Also called STRIPWORK.

ligneous

(Adj.) Wooden, actual or simulated.

lignum vitae

Hard wood suitable for carving. The best comes from the tree *Guaiacum officinale*.

limited edition

Applied to books and prints. Any edition limited to a stated number of copies.

limn(er)

Derived from the old English word *elim* and the Latin *luminare*, meaning to illuminate, originally a limner was an illustrator of medieval manuscripts, working with red pigment (*minium*), hence the word **miniatures**. The term has largely been overtaken by engravers and miniaturists although it still survives in the title of the Society of Limners (i.e. painters of miniatures), founded in 1986. The traditional appointment of Painter and Limner to the Sovereign continues.

line-and-wash

Watercolour mount enclosed within lines between which the same colour is applied as a wash.

linocut

A modern development from **wood engraving**. A relief process whereby the cuts on the linoleum appear white in a picture which is then prepared by inking the parts of the surface that have not been cut away.

linseed oil

Linseed is the seed of the flax plant. The oil extracted from the seed is the traditional binding agent for coloured paints.

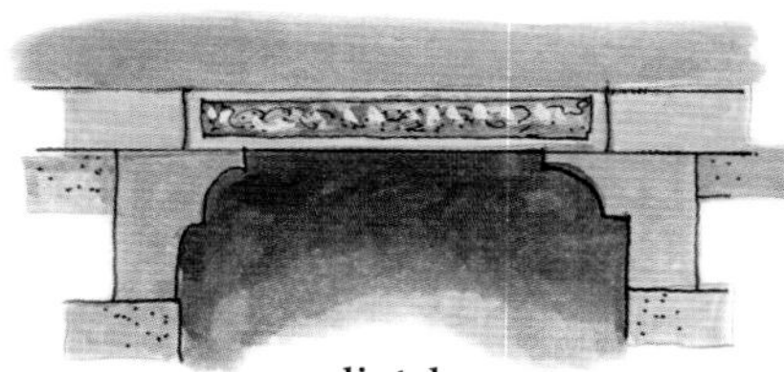

lintel

lintel

A horizontal stone or beam resting on the **jambs** of a doorway or window.

liquid madder lake

A concentrated tincture extracted from the madder plant giving a brilliant, transparent rose colour in oil and watercolour paints. Also known as **rose madder** or **rubiat**.

lith.

Indicates the engraver who drew on the stone; can also refer to the fact that the print is a **lithograph**.

lith. by

Indicates the name of the person who worked someone else's design on the stone.

lithograph

Invented in 1798 by Aloys Senefelder (1771-1834), a Bavarian dramatist who was seeking a way to duplicate his plays. Modern development of the process involves thin aluminium plates being wrapped around a cylinder before being dampened and inked alternately by rollers. OFFSET LITHOGRAPHY is when the ink image is transferred from the inking plate on to a rubber-covered transfer cylinder before being printed on to the chosen surface. PHOTO-OFFSET is when a photograph is deposited on to a specially sensitised plate, which is then processed further before printing.

Little Masters

17th century German printmakers and engravers christened thus because of the small size of their work.

livery frame

A pejorative term when the same type of frame is used to hang an entire disparate collection.

loggia
A feature of some Italian architecture where one or more sides of a building are open to the air, supported by **piers** or pillars.

Louis XIV style
A description of the arts of France during the golden age of Louis XIV (1638-1715).

lowboy
A chest of drawers with short legs.

lower table
Vide **collet**.

low relief
Vide **bas relief**.

L

lozenge
An heraldic term for a figure in which the horizontal diameter is equal to the length of the sides. Their principal use is to bear the arms of spinsters and widows when they replace more conventional shields.

lucarne
A roof window.

lumino legno
A procedure involving selective **gilding** on a dark ground in order to highlight the ornament.

lunette
A crescent shaped or semicircular space in a wall which contains a painting or statue. Also describes a similar shaped area within an arched **pediment**.

lustre
A thin metallic coating giving an irridescent glaze to **ceramics**. Also describes the effect of applying a glaze over paint or **gold leaf**. More generally, it denotes brilliancy or glossiness.

M

mace
A small form of metal tool with a spiked head used in some forms of etching and printmaking. The head varies in size and thickness according to the work required.

mace

machicolation
Openings between the **corbels** on the top walls of battlements through which lethal solids and liquids could be thrown down.

maculature
An obscure printing term applied to useless **impressions** when the ink on the plate has been weakened or absent altogether, thus removing all the lines, e.g. blotting paper.

maiolica
A kind of fine **earthenware**, decorated in colour on an opaque white glaze. Very popular, especially in Italy, between the 15th and 17th centuries. FONTANA MAIOLICA is particularly fine, coming from Urbino where the 16th century painter Orazio Fontana (1510-1571) was among the finest of the period. MEZZA MAIOLICA is an early, simpler form. Although sometimes thought as synonymous, **majolica** is an English variant of maiolica.

majolica
The English ceramicist Herbert Minton (1793-1858) developed a cane coloured **stoneware** moulded into **high relief** before being dipped into a tin enamel and fired. Thus, majolica, which originated in 1851, is the anglicised, distinctive sub-type of **maiolica**.

maker's mark
The device on silverware indicating the maker. Until the early 17th century this was a symbol, between 1696 and 1720 the first two letters of the surname appear often as a **rebus**, thereafter letters only were used within a wide variety of shields.

malachite
A vibrant green mineral used in the preparation of paint until about 1800; now used mostly for decorative purposes e.g. the Malachite Room in the Hermitage, in which is featured a fine malachite vase.

manière criblée

Also known as DOTTED PRINTS. Prints taken from a metal plate engraved as for a white-line wood block. A series of dots is punched on to the plate. Common between the mid 15th and mid 16th centuries, especially in Florence, revived in England at the end of the 18th century.

mannered

A term of criticism for a work of art thought to be affected, over-refined or inherently pompous. Not to be confused with **mannerism** which refers to the portrayal of a painter's own particular style carried to an excessive degree.

Mannerism

An Italian style of art in the 16th century, preceding the **baroque period**. When popularised by the Italian artist and author Giorgio Vasari (1511-1574), its florid, highly worked style was viewed favourably, but a century later it was in disfavour becoming seen as a decline from the High Renaissance into an undiscerning imitation of the great **masters**. The division of Mannerism into two distinct phases is now recognised, the second period beginning c1530 when the anti-classical style was further elaborated. Another meaning describes the excessive use of a painter's idiosyncratic style or mode of working.

maquette

A preliminary model for a **sculpture**, generally in wax and smaller than the intended original. Occasionally used to denote a preliminary sketch.

Maratto frame

Maratto frame

Vide **Carlo Maratto**.

marble

Soft crystallised limestone which takes many forms according to where found. The term also refers to a sculpture or any other object made from marble. Artificial marble is made from an amalgam of **alum**, **gypsum**, **isinglass**, and colouring matter. 'To marble' is also used as a verb meaning to simulate the appearance of marble.

margin

The area of a print outside the plate mark. The size of the margin can be important for dating the copy.

mark of origin

The mark on silver ware, different for each assay office, which shows where the item was assayed. First introduced in London in 1509, in Birmingham 1773, Chester 1701, Dublin 1638, Edinburgh 1552, Exeter c1570, Glasgow 1681, Newcastle c1658, Norwich 1565, Sheffield 1773, York c1560. Marks used by minor guilds date from about 1370 (Barnstaple).

marouflage
Paper oil sketches stuck down on canvas.

marquetry
A design technique applied to wood where small coloured pieces of wood are assembled and then fitted as an intrinsic part of the object, usually a piece of furniture. Not to be confused with **inlay** or **parquetry**.

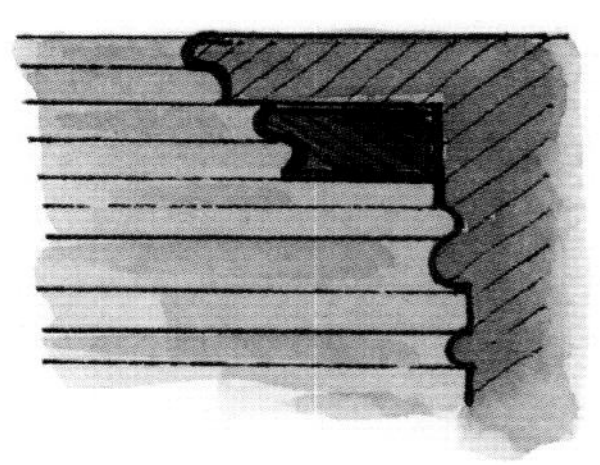
mason's mitre

mason's mitre
A corner joint where the visible and structural joints do not coincide. In **auricular** and **Sunderland** frames the stepped joint is secured by a **back frame**.

Massurrealism
A term coined by the American artist James Seehafer in 1992 to indicate painting or images extracted from electronic media based on **surrealism** and **pop art**. It is more an inchoate **genre** than a substantive movement.

master
An epithet long used by art historians, particularly to designate early engravers whose real name remains unknown. Thus the earliest recorded engraver is known as the 'Master of the Playing Cards' (c1430). Other well-known examples are the 'Master of the Year 1446', 'Master of the Garden of Love' (fl 1450), 'Master of the Berlin Passion' and 'Master of the Housebook' (fl 1480).
Vide **Old Master**.

mastic
A sticky substance extracted from the mastic tree, used to make varnish.

matt (gold)
In **water gilding**, when the unburnished gilt has an unpolished appearance, usually protected by a coat of **size** or **lacquer**. In oil painting, it is the flat finish apparent before the application of varnish.

matting punch
One method of dotting directly on to an engraver's plate by using a matting punch which, in conjunction with a hammer, can be employed for producing a crayon effect. The head of the punch is flattened and grooved like a file.

matting punch

mattoir
A printmaker's tool for the preparation of **mezzotints**. It consists of a series of spikes on a circular knob at the end of a wooden handle.

meander
An ornamental pattern of lines winding in and out, sometimes with rectangular turnings.

medium
Material used by an artist in the preparation of an original work (i.e. not a print). When more than one kind of material is used it is said to be done in **mixed media**.

medium relief
Vide **relief**.

megilp
A mixture of gum resin and **linseed** oil, used as an additive to oil paints. Most common in the 19th century. Also spelt magilp.

Meiji
The period in Japan (1868-1912) reigned over by the Emperor Meiji Tenno.

M

meiping
Chinese pottery vase whose shape is based upon the female body. Also known as a PRUNUS VASE.

Meissen
Germany's finest hard paste porcelain factory, operational since the first decade of the 18th century. Sometimes loosely referred to as DRESDEN.

memento mori
Decorative emblem of death, commonly worn and depicted in paintings in the 16th and early 17th centuries.

meniscus
A body that is concave on one side and convex on the other. Crescent-shaped. A term specifically applied to a kind of photographic lens.

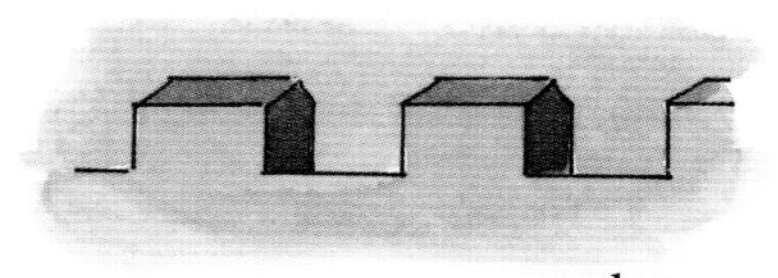
merlon

merlon
Stonework in a fortification that separates two **crenelles** or **embrasures**.

Metaphysical art
A term used by Carlo Carrá and Giorgio de Chirico for an approach to painting developed from the **Futurism movement**. Ordinary objects were presented outside their customary context, rendering them ethereal and mysterious. From their influence stemmed **Dadaism** and **Surrealism**.

metope
In architecture, a square space between **triglyphs**, i.e. a series of tablets in a **Doric frieze**. Thus in describing a frame, metope similarly refers to a space between the triglyphs in a Doric frieze. The name is derived from the Greek words for a 'hollow' and for 'between'. In early Doric architecture the metopes were left open

metope

and seen as apertures or hollows between the beams. Sometimes they were sculpted in **high relief**, sometimes left plain.

mezzotint

A method of engraving on a copper or steel plate in which the surface has been slightly roughed and then smoothed producing smooth areas where it was roughened and lighter areas where smoothed. This is the reverse direction to all other engraving procedures. The technique was invented by Ludwig von Siegen (1609-c1680) in the mid 17th century and was eventually superseded by photography.

mihrab

A niche in an inside wall of a mosque indicating the direction of Mecca, and usually housing a copy of the Koran.

millefiori

Vide **Murrini**.

miniature

A miniature painting or engraving describes a small work where the image is not more than one-sixth the size of the original subject and does not exceed 7" x 5" (17.5 x 11cm) when framed. In portraiture the head should be no more than 2" (5cm) high. Nowadays, miniatures are painted on **ivorine**, **vellum** or **paper**. Although the technique of miniature painting currently enjoys a period of resuscitation, the glories of the 17th and early 18th century works on canvas and ivory were eventually eroded by the arrival of photography. Miniatures can be divided into two categories: **cabinet miniatures**, set in frames for displaying on walls or on a flat surface, and **ornamental miniatures**, generally encased in lockets, ornamented with jewels and sometimes with the hair of the sitter framed within the reverse.

Minimalist(m)

A movement among painters and, to a greater degree, among sculptors and interior decorators, which reduces work to basic forms and structure. Impersonal in character, emphasising clarity. A leading exponent is the American sculptor Carl André (b.1935).

Minoan

Minoan

Relating to the bronze age civilisation based upon Crete which flourished c3000-1100 B.C.

mirrors

Vide **reposes**.

misericord

A bracket, or hinged seat, on the underside of a **choir** seat, often with **grotesques** carved in the **Gothic** style. Also known as a MISERERE. Other meanings are (a) a place for quiet relaxation in a monastery, and (b) a type of dagger used in the 15th century to end the misery of a badly wounded knight. Derived from *misereri* (pity) and *cor cordis* (heart).

mitre
The joint of two pieces of wood or other material at an angle of 90° such that the line of junction bisects the angle. Sometimes spelt MITER.

mitre leaf
On a frame, a large leaf covering the corner joint or mitre.

mixed media
When the materials used in a work of art are more than one kind. For example, watercolours may be combined with ink or **gouache**, or oil paint. The mediums involved are not usually identified by the artist although often they will be apparent.

mobile(s)
A modern form of sculpture or decoration which has a three dimensional shape, free moving from a suspended position.

modern art
The relevant artistic period is open to a variety of interpretations. Consensus suggests 1880, when traditional art and art forms gave way to different styles of approach and treatment. The emphasis in modern art is on form rather than content, artistic disintegration followed by repeated attempts at renewal.

monochrome
The use of only one colour in a picture, print or photograph, or when in black and white only.

monopodium
A furniture term describing a leg in the form of the head or leg of an animal, often a lion.

monotype
An engraving procedure whereby the subject is painted in oils on the surface of the plate. An impression is then made either by hand pressure or in a printing press. Called a monotype because only one impression is possible. More recent developments, developed by Sir Hubert Herkomer (1849-1914), enabled more than one impression to be taken from a plate similarly painted from a metallic mould.

monstrance
After the 14th century it became a transparent glass shrine used in the Roman Catholic Church for carrying the consecrated host before the congregation prior to being placed on the altar. Also known as an OSTENSORY or THEOTHECA.

montage
The assembly of fragments of various materials to form a meaningful composition.

monteith
A large punch bowl with a decoratively shaped fluted rim. Also used to carry wine glasses.

monteith

moonstone
Vide **feldspar**.

mordant
In printing it is a corrosive liquid, such as ***aqua fortis***, used to etch lines on a plate. Three of the most common mordants are nitric acid, dilute hydrochloric acid mixed with chlorate of potash, and perchloride of iron (the least favoured).

moresque
Complex surface decoration on a frame, often of interwoven foliage. Typical ornamentation found on **Alhambra frames**. A decorative style with flat patterns, intertwinings, and simple scrolls usually in basic colours, founded upon Moorish decoration.

morocco
Real leather from goatskin, or simulated leather, used in bookbinding. LEVANT is the most elegant and smoothest variety.

mortic(s)e-and-tenon
A joint where a projecting piece of wood (a **tenon**) on one piece of timber is fixed through a matching hole (a MORTICE) in another timber. The junction thus formed is known as a MORTICE JOINT.

mosaic
An artistic inlaid pattern made of small pieces of material, usually of hard substances, as distinct from **inlays** of wood, **ivory** or similar. The most common materials are coloured stone and glass. **Glass mosaics** are pieces of glass cut from coloured glass rods. When the glass used is of normal size it is known as **Roman mosaic**. When the pieces are smaller, usually a quarter of an inch square, the finished product is known as a **Byzantine** or **Venetian** mosaic. *Vide also* **straw mosaic**, **cloisonné mosaic**, **Florentine mosaic**.

mother-of-pearl
Irridescent inner layer of the shells of various molluscs, especially the pearl-oyster. The irridescence is caused by light passing through minute furrows in each layer. MOTHER-OF-PEARL WORK is a kind of **embroidery** using small pieces of mother-of-pearl that have been bored through with small holes and then sewn on to the fabric.

moucharaby
An enclosed balcony such that a person can see below without himself being seen. Also known as a **lattice window**.

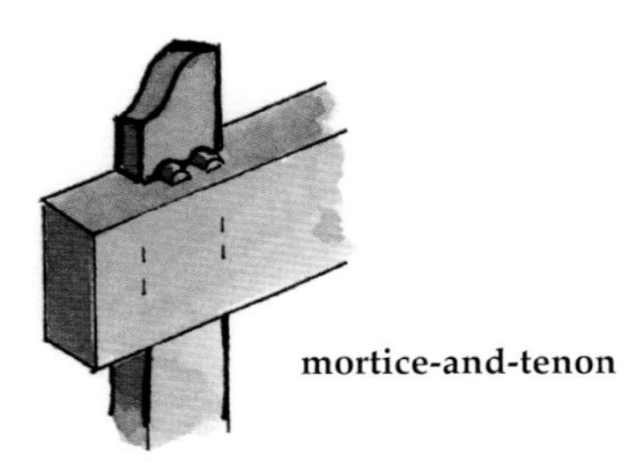
mortice-and-tenon

moulage

A little used term for a mould, impression or cast, most commonly for use as evidence in criminal investigation.

moulding

An ornamentally shaped strip of material, generally wood, to provide an outline support for a picture. It may be plain or enriched. In architecture, mouldings embellish the underside of **arches**, **bases** and **capitals**. They provide the best way of dating early large buildings, especially churches.

mount

The margin surrounding a drawing or photograph, generally of thin wood or card, often in a pale colour.

M

muffle kiln

A small box kiln for firing enamel decoration by radiation without direct exposure to the flame.

mullion

The division, usually of stone, dividing the lights of windows.

mural

A wall painting, usually in **distemper**. Some of the best known and finest examples are at Pompeii.

Murrini

A process of glass decoration first used by the Romans and rediscovered at Murano in Italy in the 16th century. It became best known as a form of Venetian glass sometimes called **millefiori** or **mosaic glass**. The glass is decorated by brightly coloured raised discs introduced within the main body of the glass.

N

nacre
An ornament for adornment having a variety of different colours. Associated with **mother-of-pearl**, hence NACRÉ (i.e. having such a lustre).

naos
An enclosed area within a classical Grecian temple wherein was placed the altar and an image of divinity.

nature print
In the 15th and 16th centuries a process was developed whereby a plant was dried and flattened, then blackened with candlewax to make impressions when laid over paper. This was later improved with the use of ink and again in the 19th century by relief impressions taken in lead and reproduced by electrotype. Commonly used to depict skeletons of ferns and seaweed.

nave
The main passageway through the middle of a church.

Nazarenes
In art history this was a group of German painters who formed what they christened the BROTHERHOOD OF ST. LUKE in 1810. Working from a disused Roman monastery their aim was to return religious painting closer to the medieval.

needle
An essential tool of the etcher, also known as an **etching needle**. A metal needle at the end of a wooden handle used for making lines on the surface of the **ground**. The point may vary in thickness and shape according to the required design.

needle

Neo-classicism
A general term describing any art form based upon classical designs and methods, especially those characteristic of ancient Greece and early Rome. At their most potent in 20th century Europe, including Russia.

Neo-impressionism
A late group of **Impressionists** who sought to bring a tighter, more scientific method to the use of colour. Leading disciples were Camille Pisarro (1830-1903), Paul Signac (1863-1935), and Georges Seurat (1859-1891).

Neo-plasticism

A form of abstract art first developed by the Dutch painter Piet Mondrian when a member of the **De Stijl** circle. From the Dutch *de nieuwe beelding* meaning new art. Art limited to squares and rectangles, only straight and horizontal or vertical lines, with primary colours or no colours.

netsuke

A finely carved **ivory** or wooden functional ornament used by the Japanese to suspend articles from the waist; pronounced 'netskee'.

newel

The central post of a spiral stair or the top or bottom support of a central stair.

Newlyn School

Influential group of ***plein air*** painters working in the late 19th century around the Cornish coastal village of Newlyn.

niellist

One who uses **niello**.

niello

A black mixture of sulphur with lead, silver or copper, used for filling lines in silver or other metal. Also used in the form of a metal inlay in some frame **mouldings**. The process originated in Italy and later became most popular in Russia.

nimbus

Vide **aureola**.

nogging

Brickwork used to fill in the spaces between wooden sections, especially in partitions. A NOGGIN is a wooden drinking vessel.

Norman style

Vide **Byzantine**.

nulling

Vide **gadrooning**.

oak leaf-and-acorn
A 17th century bunched leaf type frame embellished with bunches of oak leaves.

obelisk
In art, obelisk has two meanings:
(a) a tapering rectangular **column**, and
(b) a sign in printing like a small DAGGER, by which it is also known.

obiche
A fine grained light coloured hardwood from the *Triplochiton escleroxylon* tree of West Africa. Other names by which it is known are ABACHI, OBECHI, SAMBA (Ivory Coast), AGONS (Cameroon), ARERE, WARRA (Ghana). Commonly used in furniture and for statuette carvings.

ocarina
An egg shaped porcelain object.
Also a small flute-like musical instrument.

ochre
A durable mineral of clay and ferrous oxide used in the production of both oil and watercolour paints, particularly for yellow, red and brown pigments.

octastyle
A building with eight **columns**.

oculus
The circular centre of an ornament.
An eye or leaf-bud, hence an OCULUS CATI is a ringed sapphire (asteria).

odalisque
The depiction of a female figure, modelled on that of a female slave or concubine, originally from the harems of Turkey.

oeil-de-boeuf
A circular or ovoid window.

oeuvre
The work(s) of an artist, or follower, painting (or in the case of literature, writing) in a similar idiosyncratic style.

offset
The term has two quite different meanings.
(1) A process used in the second half of the 19th century for coloured multi-printing, employing a series of cylinders.
(2) The accidental transfer of print in a book from a page of text or an illustration to the opposite page, most serious when an illustration is affected.

offset lithography

Vide **lithography**.

ogee

An architectural term to describe an s-shaped curve. Commonly used to describe such a shape in rooftops, silverware and picture frames. An OGEE-PLANE is a carpentry tool for making ogee-shaped **mouldings**.

oil gilding

A process of **gilding** in which **gold leaf** is laid on a surface prepared by a coat of **size** made from boiled **linseed oil** and **chrome yellow**, applied with a brush. When the oil has dried until slightly tacky, the leaf is applied. Chrome yellow is added to render the gold more brilliant.

oils

Generic term for paint used by artists, the ground colour pigment being mixed with oil to provide permanency, especially when protected by a varnish overcoat.

okimono

A Japanese carving, slightly larger than a **netsuke**, used as a personal adornment, or a quite small figurative ornamental object.

Old Master

European painters of the 13th-17th centuries commonly regarded as great. In recent times the term has become diluted to describe any recorded painter of olden times, conventionally between c1300 and 1800.

oleograph

A **lithographic** print made to resemble an oil painting, usually produced on canvas and having a shiny texture. Common in Victorian times.

omnium

Vide **whatnot**.

opal(ine)

A pale bluish-white mineral seen of differing shades according to variations of light. Opaline is the adjectival form; OPALINE GLASS is semi-translucent and whitened by the addition of phosphate of lime or other chemicals.

optic(al) art

A version of **abstract art** common in Britain in the 1960s whereby optical illusions of light and movement are created by the use of flat patterns of dots, lines and squares. Main proponents were Bridget Riley (1931-), and the Hungarian painter Victor Vasarely (1908-1997).

order

In Christian theology there are nine grades of celestial beings, the first two and the last two of which are often to be seen in early paintings. They are in order, **seraphim**, cherubim, thrones, dominations, principalities, powers, virtues, arch angels and angels.

ordinaries

In heraldry, the most common figures (**charges**) borne on a coat of arms. Most often used are the CHIEF, the PALE,

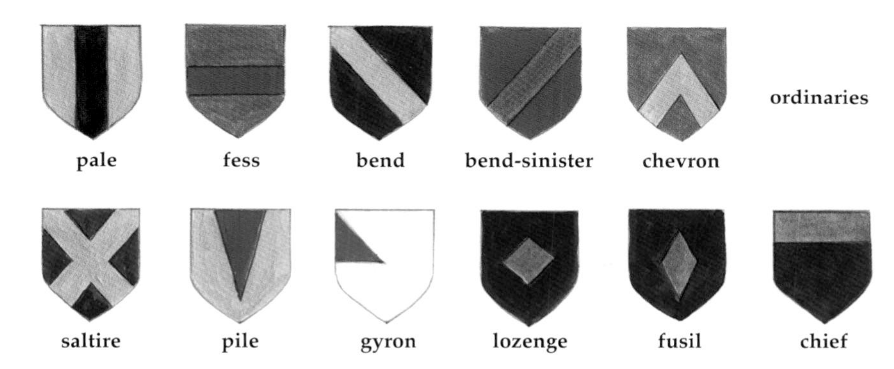

the FESS, the BEND, the BEND-SINISTER, the CHEVRON, the **saltire**, the PILE, the GYRON, the **lozenge**, and the FUSIL. In art, some royal offices, e.g. Sculptor in Ordinary to the Queen, the term denotes permanency.

organic

In art this decribes an uneven or irregular shape with angular or curved edges as in vegetable forms.

oriel

A bay window above ground level. Also describes any recess built outward above ground level.

Oriental carpets & rugs

Generally classified according to their place of origin. There are five main groups: **Iranian**, the largest and most important group; **Turkoman**, the well-known red carpets; **Caucasian**, the Russian group, often incorporating geometric shapes; **Turkish** or **Anatolian**; and the **Indian**, **Pakistani** and **Chinese** group. Prayer rugs are known as **kelim**, a term which also applies to any rug that is not knotted but woven without a **pile**.
Vide **Ghiordes** and **Senneh** knots.
(The map overleaf shows the main centres with the names by which the rugs and carpets made there are known.)

O

original

In painting this refers to a genuine work by the artist to whom it is attributed.
In printing it refers to any number of prints for which the **engraver** or **etcher** created the design. A full definition, intended for legal purposes, has been prepared by Unesco, reprinted in 1965. The basic essentials are a) the artist alone has created the master image in or upon the plate, stone, wood block or other material for the purpose of creating the print; b) the print is made from the matrix by the artist or following his directions; and c) the finished print is approved by the artist.

Oriental carpets

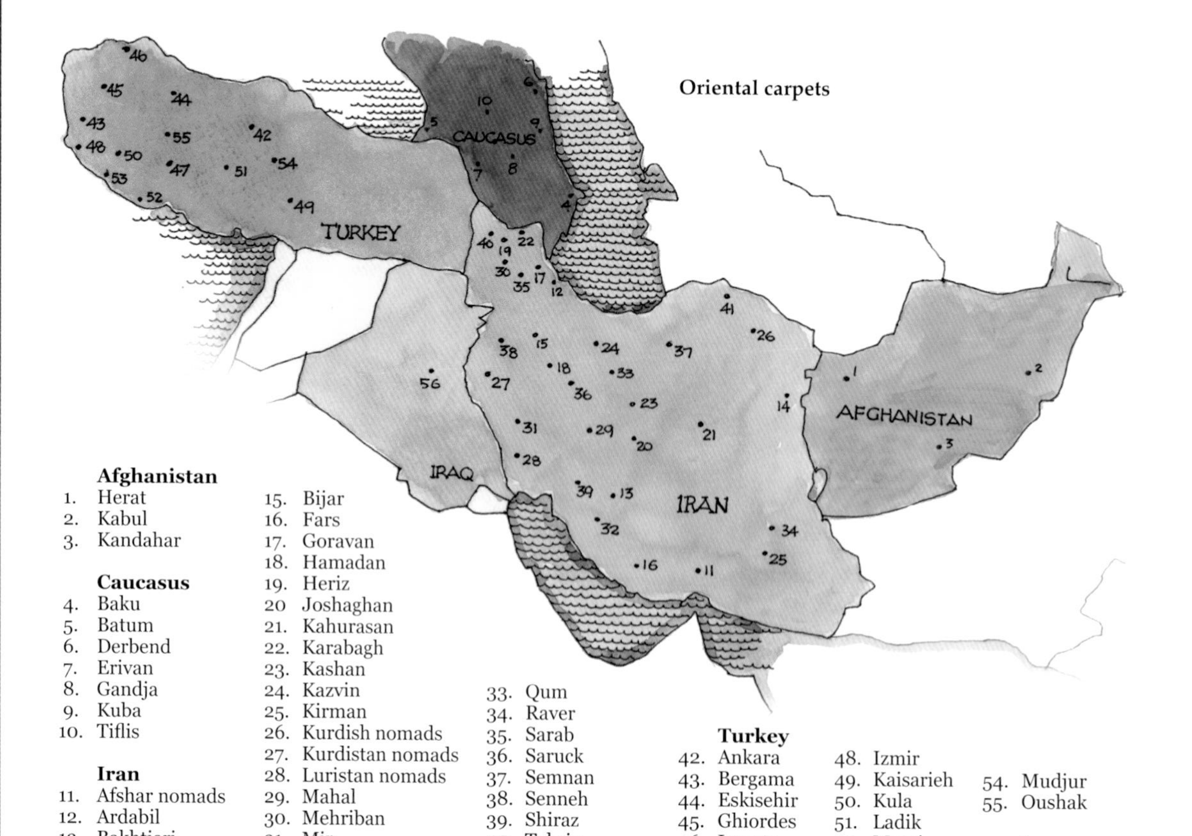

Afghanistan
1. Herat
2. Kabul
3. Kandahar

Caucasus
4. Baku
5. Batum
6. Derbend
7. Erivan
8. Gandja
9. Kuba
10. Tiflis

Iran
11. Afshar nomads
12. Ardabil
13. Bakhtiari
14. Baluchi nomads
15. Bijar
16. Fars
17. Goravan
18. Hamadan
19. Heriz
20 Joshaghan
21. Kahurasan
22. Karabagh
23. Kashan
24. Kazvin
25. Kirman
26. Kurdish nomads
27. Kurdistan nomads
28. Luristan nomads
29. Mahal
30. Mehriban
31. Mir
32. Qashgai nomads
33. Qum
34. Raver
35. Sarab
36. Saruck
37. Semnan
38. Senneh
39. Shiraz
40. Tabriz
41. Tekke nomads

Turkey
42. Ankara
43. Bergama
44. Eskisehir
45. Ghiordes
46. Isparta
47. Istanbul
48. Izmir
49. Kaisarieh
50. Kula
51. Ladik
52. Megri
53. Melas
54. Mudjur
55. Oushak

Iraq
56. Baghdad

ormolu
A gold coloured **alloy** of copper, zinc and tin, used mainly as an embellishment on fine furniture and clocks.

ornamental miniature
Vide **miniature**.

Orphism
A branch of **cubism** in which colours were used without reference to anything in the conventional world. A group of French painters, led by Robert Delaunay (1885-1941) and Fernand Léger (1881-1955), called themselves *La Section d'Or* in contrast to more austere cubists such as Braque and Picasso.

orrery
A decorative rotating model of the solar system operated by clockwork, the best examples, which vary in size and shape, being made of brass and quality wood.

orthoclase
Aluminium and potassium silicate, a common **feldspar**, used in making pottery.

ovolo
A rounded or convex **moulding** seen in section as a quarter of a circle.

Oxford India paper
Vide **India paper**.

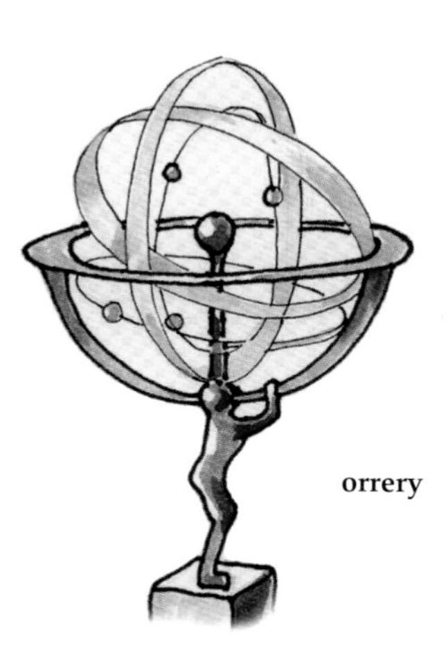

orrery

P

painterly
Originally used to distinguish between **baroque** and **renaissance** art, it has come to describe work which demonstrates the masterly use of paint.

Pakistani carpets
Vide **Oriental carpets**.

paktong
A whitish alloy of copper, nickel, and zinc used in the manufacture of domestic objects during the latter part of the 18th century. When polished can be mistaken for silver. First used by the Chinese, hence its name. Also called **German silver**.

palette
A wooden or plastic object upon which a painter lays his oils, generally in a specific colour order. The conventional woods used are mahogany and walnut. Palette can also refer to the range of colours characteristically used by a particular artist. Not to be confused with PALATE (taste), nor with PALETTES (the armoured plates shielding the junction of shoulders and arms on a coat of armour).

palette knife
A thin blunt triangular steel blade with a handle used by painters in oils to apply, mix or remove paint.

palimpsest
A base for handwriting, usually paper or parchment, on which original writing has been removed to allow other writing to appear upon it. The term also applies to a monumental brass re-engraved on the reverse side.

paliotto
The painting at the front of an Italian altar piece.

Palladian
The neo-classical style of the Italian architect Andrea Palladio (1518-1580). In architecture it applies to a phase in Britain from about 1715, a reaction to **baroque**, rekindling the influence of Palladio and Inigo Jones (1573-1652). It also refers to a **Kent frame** in the Palladian style, popular in the 19th century, but the style has many variations.

P

palladium
An image or statue of the mythological goddess Pallas. The myth is that the safety of Troy depended upon its preservation.

palmette
An ornamental shape of radiating petals reminiscent of a palm leaf.

panel frame
Common around the turn of the 17th century, having panels between running foliage ornamentation. A panel also refers to a hard smooth surface, generally of wood, used for painting in oil, especially in the 18th and 19th centuries.

paniconography
A commercial method, similar to **zincography**, for producing a design in **relief** on a zinc ground before printing in a press.

pantheon
A temple to all the gods, specifically the pantheon in Rome, dating from the early 2nd century. Popularised to describe any collection of greatness, whether of people or institutions.

pantograph
An instrument used in buildings, engravings and sculpture to reduce the size of an original cast or plan. It involves a complex system of jointed rods consisting of four perforated arms arranged in pairs and jointed together where they cross and where they meet at the top and bottom of their respective Vs. For curved figures a modification is needed known as a POLAR PANTOGRAPH whereby two arms are supported in a light frame and united by a rack on each and a common pinion such that the movement of one arm controls that of the other.

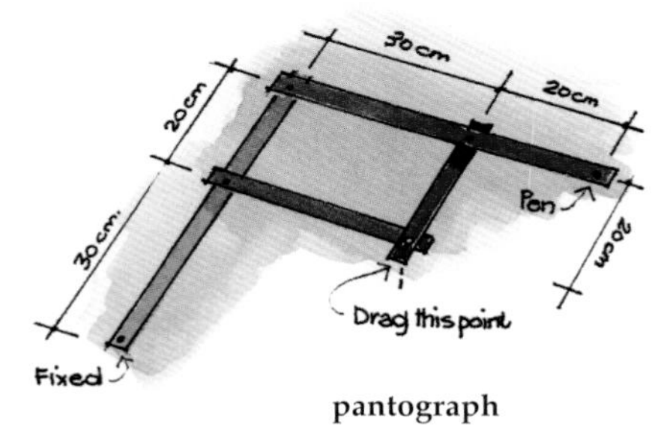

pantograph

pantone
A pre-mixed colour of which there are more than three thousand examples, each with its own numbered **CMYK**. The name derives from the American founding company of the same name.

paper
Variations in the manufacture of paper down the centuries facilitates the dating of paper when used for painting or print-making. Before the 19th century paper was handmade, sheet by sheet, from fibres reduced in water to a pulp. Machinery was first used in England in 1801. Cheap quality paper, **cordage**, was made from old tarred ropes, while good quality was made from linen or cotton rags. In the 18th century, artists and printmakers distinguished between **cartoon** paper and the more ordinary paper used for printing books.

Writing paper was surface-dipped in a gelatinous solution made from either white soap and powdered **alum** or glue, resinous soap, alum, and paper pulp. *Vide* **watermarks**.

papier collé
A form of collage, using coloured paper, first used by Georges Braque (1882-1963).

papier-mâché
Paper pulp used for moulding in to boxes, trays, etc. When soaked in a binder, used for making ornaments on frame moulds. The finest kind is processed by pasting together many sheets of a particular kind of pulp, used in the making of trays and similar objects where strength is required. Occasionally used in picture framing, most often in the mid 18th century, and revived a century later.

parapet
The edge of a wall projecting above roof level.

P

parcel gilt
Partly gilded silver plate; used to describe gilt highlights against a plain ground.

Parian ware
Derived from the island of Paros, it refers to both white PARIAN MARBLE found there and, more commonly, to a kind of white porcelain. *Vide* **Belleek**.

parquetry
The making and use of small wooden blocks of various types or colours so arranged as to form a mosaic design which are then inlaid for flooring or furniture. Not to be confused with **inlay** or **marquetry**.

parterre
Garden flower beds set in a level, formal manner.

Pasitelean
Relating to an important school of Greek sculpture founded by Pasiteles (1st century B.C.) in Rome.

pastel
Powdered pigments bound with gum to produce a **crayon**. Can also refer to a drawing done in pastel.

pastel manner
A succession of plates used in the preparation of a coloured **etching** which when printed simulates pastel.

pastiche
A work of art or musical composition rendered in the style of another. Also known as a PASTICCIO. Not to be confused with **fake** or **forgery**.

pastiglia
Gesso ornament, either produced from a mould or roughly brushed.

pâte de verre
A very early process of glassmaking, dating back to the 2nd century B.C., although the name, which literally means 'glass paste', was first applied by the French in the 19th century after its revival following

archaeological discoveries in Egypt. The technique involves converting crushed glass into a powder and binding it into a paste. This is then pasted on to a mould and fired in an extremely hot kiln. Used in the making of **mosaics** and fine glass objects, the technique was rendered obsolete by the arrival of glass blowing.

pâte sur pâte

Ceramic term for decoration by either fine enamel or porcelain paste upon a prepared surface so as to produce a very **low relief**. The finest examples are pure white whereas works of lesser quality have a grey tint.

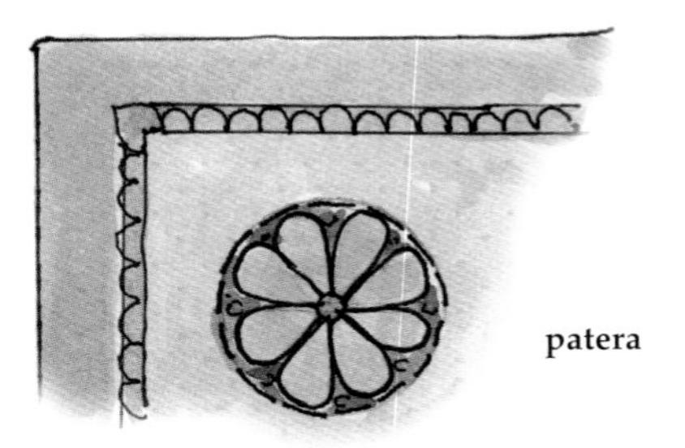

patera

patera

Radially symmetrical floral ornament, sometimes stylised, carved in **low relief**, often surrounding a **central boss**. Originally the ornament was saucer-shaped, hence the name, but it soon came to encompass other forms such as rosettes.

patina

A gloss on wooden surfaces produced by age. May also apply to metal when it refers to the effects of specific treatment, as for example in bronze ware after exposure to the weather or prolonged burial. Darkened patina on bronze can be produced artificially by the application of various acids, although such disfigurement should be avoided.

pearl

A small pearl-like bead often repeated as a series usually running along the **sight edge** of a frame.

pedestal

The part of a **column** below the **base**. In **tabernacle frames** the pedestal usually stands forward of the base.

pediment

The triangular front of a classical building in **baroque** or **mannerist** style. Also the top element in a **tabernacle frame**.

peel

Defensive square towerhouse originating in the Scottish borders in the 16th century and beyond. Also spelled PELE.

Pegasus

A mythological winged horse said to have come from the blood of Medusa when Perseus cut off her head.

Pembroke table

A light table with collapsible flaps, differing from a **sofa table** by the shape of the top when opened. The most popular form is in satinwood, dating from the 1770s. Sheraton asked for the height to be no more than 28", including castors.

pen work

A form of **japanned** furniture ornament using **Indian ink** made to simulate an etching. Patterns throughout the 19th century were prepared by designers using a lead pencil on strong paper which were then copied onto the furniture.

pendant

Hanging down (*adj*). A hanging rather than fixed piece of jewellery (*n*).

pentimento(i)

Signs of earlier work showing through an oil painting on canvas. Most common among the works of the early masters. The term is derived from the Italian for 'repentance'. Sometimes referred to as PENTIMENTS.

penumbra

When applied to a painting it refers to an almost imperceptible boundary between light and shade.

P

performance art

A 20th century form of visual activity, aimed as an art form, in which the performance of an individual or group of individuals is the focus.

peristyle

Area of a large building or church surrounded by a range of columns.

Perpendicular style

A style of English medieval architecture popular 1350-1550. Its principal characteristics are the use of straight horizontals and verticals, with the straight lines of its **tracery** intersecting at right angles.

Perpendicular architecture

Persian knot

Vide **Senneh knot**.

perspective

The perceived spatial relationship of objects. In painting this can refer either to the artist's depiction of spatial relationships in his work or to the mental attitude held by the artist or viewer.

pewter

A grey **alloy** of tin, copper and **antimony**, usually limited to four parts of tin to one of lead. Used mainly for table ware of lesser quality, the best and many older examples carry a **maker's mark**. When made without lead it is known as **Britannia metal**.

photo-offset

Vide **lithography**.

photorealism
An art movement of the mid 20th century, a reaction against **abstract art**, concentrating on everyday scenes depicted in a photographic and detailed manner. In sculpture it is commonly referred to as **superrealism**. From it stemmed **hyperrealism**.

piedroit
A square pillar projecting from the front of a wall. It differs from a **pilaster** as being without a **base** or a **capital**.

pier
In a frame, an unsupported **column** having a square section. *Vide* **pilaster**.

pietra dura
Ornamental work in **inlay** of hard stones such as **agates** and **jaspers**, especially when on a large scale. The term is derived from the Italian *pier* and *dura*, meaning hard stone.

pigment
Any material which provides colour to a drawing or painting. Also used to describe the natural colour in animals and plants. When pigment is mixed with dry colouring material and moistened it becomes paint.

pilaster
A rectangular column often projecting from a wall. In early Italianate frames it refers to an engaged **pier**, i.e. a solid area between openings.

pile
Applied to floor coverings, the pile is the soft projecting surface of the material. *Vide* **Ghiordes** and **Senneh knots**.

pinchbeck
A copper and zinc alloy in nearly equal parts having a slightly golden appearance, used mainly in the production of cheap jewellery and inlaid work. Also used to describe something false or **counterfeit**.

pinnacle
The topmost point of a building. By adding weight to what is immediately beneath, it strengthens a spire against lateral forces.

pinx(it)
Appearing after an artist's name means 'he/she painted it'.

piqué
The term was first applied to tortoiseshell decoration with gold points known as PIQUÉ D'OR. Now the name is given to similar work in silver and on **ivory**, POSÉ D'OR, or CLOUTÉ D'OR. Not to be confused with **mother-of-pearl**.

pitchwai
Indian temple hangings, generally tapestry.

'Pitti Palace' frames
A 20th century revival based on a common Italian 17th century style. Refers to the Palazzo Pitti, seat of the Medici family in Florence, wherein is housed the great Palatine Gallery collection of mainly **Renaissance** art.

plagiarism
The use of another's ideas or work passed off as one's own. Because members of one school of art often build upon the developments of another artist, period or school, the use of the term demands careful interpretation. *Vide* **cartoon** and **cartouche**.

plaque
An ornamental plate or badge usually of metal, porcelain or wood. Small versions are known as PLAQUETTES.

plaster of Paris
The same as **Gesso**.

plateresque
Reminiscent of silverware.
A seldom used architectonic adjective.

point
Vide **carat**.

P

pointillism
A method of accentuating light and shade by using combinations of primary colours in a mosaic of dots or small areas of paint, perfected by the French Impressionist painter Georges Seurat (1859-1891). When viewed from a distance the colours blend, accentuating luminosity. Also known as **divisionism**.

polar pantograph
Vide **pantograph**.

pole
The laborious process of using the **rocker** when preparing the **ground** for an **engraving** is lessened when a long pole handle is attached to the rocker enabling it to oscillate in all directions.

pontil
In glass-making a pontil is an iron rod used for revolving the soft glass as it is being formed. The mark left at the base is the PONTIL MARK.

Pop art
Art based on the modern media and culture. It has been thought of as **Dadaism** brought up to date. Although viewed by some as derisory, for its proponents in the mid and late 20th century it was intended to bring together established art and its contemporary banal cousins. Especially associated with the artists Andy Warhol (1928-1987), Roy Lichtenstein (1923-1997), and Jasper Johns (b. 1930).

porcelain
A hard vitrified translucent ceramic made from a collation of **feldspar**, **kaolin** (porcelain clay) and silica. There are three main types according to composition and treatment: (i) HARD PASTE, made primarily from kaolin combined with material such as ground white sand, with a glaze made similarly; (ii) SOFT PASTE, with a hard glaze, of varied composition to simulate early Oriental hard paste porcelain; (iii) MIXED PORCELAIN, similar to soft paste but containing a degree of kaolin. Best known examples of hard paste porcelain are early Oriental wares, Meissen, post 1770 Sèvres, Bristol, Lowestoft and New Hall; examples of soft paste are pre 1770 Sèvres and most British factories; medieval Italian

products and many of the lesser modern European factories are of the hybrid variety, hard to distinguish from soft paste.

porch

Covered entrance over the doorway to a building.

pornography

Vide **erotica**.

porphyry

A dark mineral or rock, much favoured by the early Egyptians, excelling other marbles in its response to polish. It has an attractive dark red-coloured ground.

porringer

Originally, a dish for porridge. A small bowl with a single handle.

portfolio

A case for carrying loose sheets of drawings. Hence a collection of an artist's work as used, for example, by an artist or his agent when visiting potential buyers.

portico

A **colonnade**. A **porch** or open vestibule at the entrance to a building.

portrait shape

A painting or frame in which the height is greater than the width. *Vide* **landscape shape**.

poster

A large print, usually coloured and generally used for advertising hoardings. Collectors distinguish between 'originals' and 'copies', the former referring to the first impression printing. With growth in demand, copies have become more frequent and recognising the difference more important.

Post-Impressionism

An evolving movement developed from **Impressionism** led by Cézanne, van Gogh and Gauguin. Although so different in their character and form these artists separately helped to refine the naturalism which had inspired Impressionism, re-introducing form as a vital adjunct to colour while recognising the value of symbolism and content.

potiche

A rounded jar or vase with a short neck.

potichomania

Decorating the inside of a glass vase with paper or linen designs.

potpourri

A covered jar for holding potpourri, which traditionally comprised dried rose petals and a variety of spices. More generally, the term refers to richly enamelled pottery of the 18th century.

potsherd

A fragment of broken ceramics. Most commonly refers to archaeological finds.

potstone

Vide **soapstone**.

potter's wheel

A revolving disc used to carry clay in the making of **pottery**. First known to have been used in the 4th millenium B.C., the technique reached Britain in the mid 1st century B.C.

pottery

Any object made from fired clay. There are three main types: **earthenware**, **porcelain**, and **stoneware**. Although largely mechanised during and after the industrial revolution, it has recently enjoyed a resurgence among individual craftsmen and women.

pouf(fe)

A firm cushion, often covered in red or brown leather, used as a footstool or low seat.

pouncet box

A small container with a perforated lid or top for storing perfume.

poussinisme

The belief that form is more important than colour in painting.

P

precious stones

The most most beautiful and valuable of **gems**. Strictly, it applies only to diamonds, rubies, emeralds and sapphires, but opals are sometimes included.

predella

An altar step or raised shelf for supporting a painting or sculpture. In a **tabernacle frame** it is the area between the **pedestals** often decorated with paintings or **reliefs**.

premium

Most European and American auction houses now charge a buyer what is euphemistically called a premium, the amount of which varies from one auction house to another and may be on a sliding scale according to the value of the purchase. A few auction houses only charge a premium for items sold above a certain figure.

Pre-Raphaelite

The Pre-Raphaelite Brotherhood was a group of English painters who, in the mid 19th century, sought to return to the directness and simplicity of early Italian painting before the age of Raphael. The leading figures were Sir Edward Burne-Jones (1833-1898), William Holman Hunt (1827-1910), Sir John Everett Millais (1829-1896), and Gabriel Dante Rossetti (1828-1882). Compositions were often biblical and figurative, painted in a bright, colourful style with close attention to detail.

primary colour(s)

Those colours - blue, red and yellow - from which all other colours are derived. They cannot be resolved in to other colours and when mixed with one another form **secondary colours**.

priming

In painting, the first coating on the canvas or board of a substance aimed at retaining unblemished paint.

Primitivism

A form of painting which seeks to return to that exemplified in primitive societies, with naive or instinctual expression.

A Frenchman, Henri Rousseau (1844-1910), was the prime exponent, although he only began painting after retirement and his works of fantasy did not become fully appreciated until after his death. His style was also called NÄIVE ART. Not to be confused with **Italian Primitives**.

print
Any illustration that is an **engraving**, an etching, or any form of photographic or computer generated reproduction.

prion
Vide **mortice**.

Progressive Art Movement
An Indian art movement founded in 1947 by Francis Newton Souza (1924-2002) and Sayed Haider Raza (b. 1927). Their aim was to paint in their own respective styles without reference to content, concerned only with what they called 'plastic coordination and colour composition'. Although the group disbanded in 1956, the commercial value of the best examples remains strong.

pronaos
An open area in an ancient temple in front of the **naos** or **cella**.

Prussian blue
A pigment made from iron and cyanogen (the base of Prussic acid). Greenish blue in colour it is much used by watercolour painters, often mixed with various proportions of white to give green hues.

psychedelic art
Any form of modern art inspired by the used of hallucinogenic drugs. It became a popular art movement in the 1960s, closely related to psychedelic rock music. The content is phantasmagoric, with strong, vivid colour and bold design. The term, literally 'mind manifesting', was first coined by the British psychiatrist Humphrey Osmond (1917-2004).

punching
The use of a fine punch for making a form of decoration on a wooden surface having had an application of **gesso** and been gilded.

purdonium
A trade name for an ordinary metal lined coal scuttle, dating from 1847.

Purism
A movement of art which sought to rid itself, after **Cubism**, of unnecessary detail and irrelevant association. Founded by the French painter Amédée Oliphant (1886-1966), the architect Charles Le Corbusier (1887-1965), and the Romanian animal sculptor Constantin Brancusi (1876-1957).

purlin
A horizontal beam running along the length of a roof.

putti
Young naked children as represented in much **Renaissance** art.

Q

quaich
A Scottish shallow drinking bowl, generally of silver, with a wide flat handle on each side. Intended mainly for whisky.

quarter bound
A book with a leather spine, but leather nowhere else. *Vide* **half bound**.

quartz
A mineral form of **silica**.

quatrefoil
A four pointed or four leaved figure resembling a clover leaf. In a frame it refers to a four lobed aperture.

quattrocento
The characteristics of Italian 15th century art, especially in painting and sculpture.

quoin
The external angle of a building. Also applied to a wedge-shaped stone, or piece of metal or wood, often used to support a stone. In printing, a quoin is a short blunt wedge used to support the **types** in a **chase** or on a **galley**.

R

rabbet
A step-shaped channel cut along the edge or face of a piece of wood, usually to receive the edge or tongue of another piece. Synonymous with **rebate**.

raffle leaf
A **bolection frame** ornamented with raffle leaves, popular in the late 17th century. The term RAFFLE refers to a leaf with serrated edges, probably derived from the French *érafler*, to graze.

rafter
A sloping beam supporting a roof.

rail
The curving top edge of a **rococo frame**.

raking knull
On the top edge of a frame, an angled pattern of ridges, often in the form of **gadrooning**. A **knull** or **astragal** is a small semi-circular **moulding** around the top of a **column**.

Raku
From the Japanese word for 'enjoyment', raku is a form of lead-glazed **earthenware** with irregular colours and surfaces caused by a method of firing whereby the pottery is removed early from the kiln and placed on a covered bed of combustible materials. Used for ritual tea drinking ceremonies.

ramin
A light coloured fine grained Malaysian hardwood used in framing.

rampant
In heraldry, standing upright on hind legs.

Rayonism
A variety of abstract painting developed in 1911 by the Russian painter Michael Larionov (1881-1964). This involved placing light spots and dark rays in juxtaposition.

Realism
A movement in art, founded in the 1850s by the French artist Gustave Courbet (1819-1877), which sought to paint the natural scene in the artist's own way without recourse to the customs and manners of earlier times. In addition to Corbet the other leading artist in the movement was Edouard

Manet (1832-1883), sometimes spoken of as the first modern painter. The movement was overtaken in 1870 by the emergence of its natural evolutionary successor, **Impressionism**.

rebate

In framing, the recess beneath the **sight edge** designed to hold the picture.

rebus

The representation of a name pictorially. In heraldry it is a device suggesting a name. Used also in early silver to indicate the maker.

reduce(d)

Bronze sculptures are sometimes reproduced from the original cast in smaller size. The reduced size is made with the help of a **pantograph**, often carrying an inscription on the base 'reduced'.

reeding

Ridged **mouldings** comprising a run of thin, convex ornaments resembling bundles of reeds tied by a ribbon or curly leaf.

R

Reformation

Of marginal influence in the development of the graphic arts, the Reformation refers to the movement led by Martin Luther in 1517 attacking what he saw as the entrenched bureaucracy and rigidity of the Roman Catholic Church.

Régence

A French type of frame in the baroque style of the Regency (1715-1723) of Philippe d'Orleans.

regency

The period when George, Prince of Wales, governed Britain as Prince Regent, 1811-1820. When used to described the style of this period, Regency refers mainly to architecture. In the graphic arts there was a revival in the use of Greek and Roman motifs and an ornate quality seen most strikingly in the picture frames of the period, reflecting a corresponding style in furniture. Not to be confused with ***Régence***.

register

When several blocks or plates are used in succession to produce a single coloured print it is necessary to ensure that the plates correspond precisely in colour and outline. Methods of ensuring this are known generically as the register.

relief

When a carved **moulding** brings a design above the surface of the work. **High relief** is when the projection is greater than the object depicted; **medium relief** when a sculpture is half raised from the slab; **low relief** is when the projection is proportionally less than the object depicted.

relief printing

A form of engraving where the lines or spaces are engraved as negatives leaving the design in **relief**. Mainly used in the preparation of wood and metal cuts. Also known as SURFACE PAINTING. The opposite of **intaglio**.

relining
Renewal of a damaged or worn canvas by the introduction of a new lining. A skilled operation only to be attempted by a qualified painting restorer.

reliquary
An object designed to hold religious objects. This may take various forms, from the richly decorated or elaborate statuaries to very simple types. Often used as altar furniture.

remarque (proof)
A print which has a small design or note in the margin of the plate, originally used by an etcher for testing his plate. Contrary to what some printsellers aver, such a mark adds no intrinsic value.

Rembrandt print
Good quality coloured prints made towards the end of the 19th century and the beginning of the 20th century by the Rembrandt Intaglio Printing Company of Lancaster.

Renaissance
An artistic and literary flourish of fresh vision and thinking which reached its creative peak between 1400 and 1600. Historical analysis distinguishes several closely related types: the Renaissance in Florence, in Rome, in Northern Europe, in France, and in Britain. Its birth was in Florence where there was a revival of interest in classical forms with a close affinity to the natural world. From the end of the 15th century the movement became known as the **High Renaissance** with Rome and Venice joining Florence at the epicentre, the time of Leonardo da Vinci (1452-1519), Michaelangelo (1475-1564), Sandro Botticelli (1445-1510), Benvenuto Cellini (1500-1571) and Scorzio Raffaello [Raphael] (1483-1520). When eventually it crystallised to become an aesthetic ritual, corruption and decadence followed. There followed the birth of **Mannerism**.

reposes
Undecorated areas in a picture frame between the carving in centre-corner pattern frames. When gilded they reflect light more than the surrounding parts and are therefore called **mirrors**.

repoussé
Metal work which has been hammered on the reverse side to produce a raised **relief**.

representational
Said of art which accurately represents the image normally seen, as in landscape or still life composition. A pejorative synonym is PHOTOGRAPHIC.

reredos
The back of a fireplace. Also a screen or ornamented space behind an altar or shrine.

resin
A generic term for organic secretions, most often from plants, with many useful applications.

retrochoir
The area in a church behind or beyond the **choir**.

retroussage
An unusual printing procedure whereby, to soften the overall effect, fine muslin is passed over the plate, gently touching the surface. This catches part of the ink so that, when drawn a little upwards, a softer quality to the lines is produced. Similarly, ink can be drawn out of the lines, producing an even **tint**.

return-bead
Vide **bead** and **reel**.

reverse section
A frame with the most prominent **moulding** nearest the picture.

rhodonite
A rose-red mineral, sometimes used as an ornamental stone.

ribbed vault
A type of vault common from the end of the 11th century when transverse ribs were introduced. This kind of vaulting comprised arches of stone from each **pillar** to a **corbel** in the outer wall, separating each compartment of the vault into a square or oblong crossed by diagonal **groins**.

ribbon-and-stick
A framing device consisting of a thin twisted **flute** around a narrow dowel or headless piece of wood. Often seen next to the top or **sight edge** of a **Maratta frame**.

rice paper
A very thin edible paper used by artists for delicate work in **gouache** or **watercolour**. Made from rice straw. It is commonly but erroneously applied to a delicate white film made from the pith of a Chinese shrub (*Fatsia papyrifera*), and from the pith of the sea shore shrub (*Scaevola koenignii*) of India, Malaysia and Australia.

ridge-piece
The ridge in a roof into which rafters are fixed.

ring
An illegal group of prospective buyers at auction, usually dealers, who delegate one of their number to bid on behalf of all. Items successfully purchased are then subjected to a private auction within the group, called a SETTLEMENT or KNOCK-OUT; when, as expected, this results in an increased final sale price, the original bidder is recompensed and the balance, called the DIVIDEND, shared equally

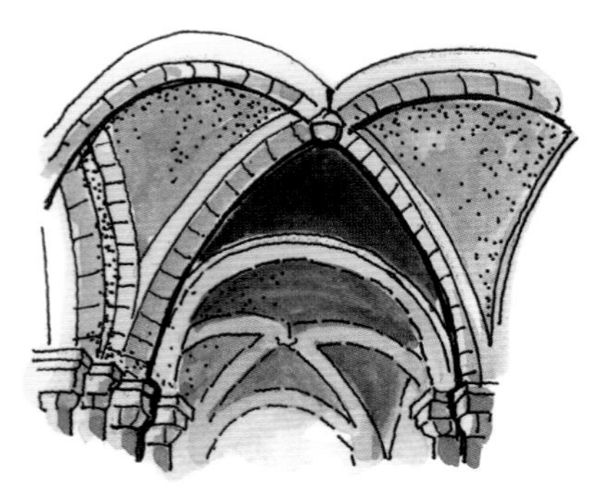

ribbed vault

among the group. Any member who seldom or never buys at the knock-out but who continually profits from the dividend becomes *persona non grata*.

ring punch

A tool used mainly by gold and silversmiths for preparing the **ground**. It is a punch with a circular, hollow head.

ringer

Dealers' slang for an object which is similar or can be mistaken for another, more valuable, item. *Vide* **sleeper**.

ripple moulding

A fine ripple, generally applied in several bands on a moulding. The style is well suited to early portraits being frequently used on Dutch and German ebonised frames of the 17th century.

rocaille

An 18th century type of ornamentation based on rock and shell motifs. A common asymmetrical decoration on **rococo** frames.

rock crystal

A generic term for all transparent quartz crystals. Rock crystal engraving on glass achieved great popularity in the late 18th century.

rocker

An instrument with a curved serrated edge for preparing a plate for **etching** or **line engraving**. Called a rocker because with the blade held at right angles to the plate the curved edge is rocked systematically over the surface at varying angles producing a uniformly indented surface.

rococo

A style of architecture, design and painting following **baroque**. Highly ornamented and florid. The style flourished principally in France, southern Germany and Austria in the first half of the 18th century. In painting its main exponents were François Boucher (1703-1770), Jean-Henri Fragonard (1732-1806), Giovanni Tiepolo (1696-1770) and Jean-Antoine Watteau (1684-1721).

roller

Implement for applying ink to a printing plate. Developed in the early 19th century to replace leather balls which became quickly worn.

roller press

A cylindrical press used for printing from **intaglio** plates. The process is a delicate one involving moving the plates horizontally on a **roller** before being placed under another steel roller, the pressure being adjusted by screws. The plate is then heated, inked and wiped, replaced on to a bed and then covered with damp paper and dry absorbent material. It is then passed slowly and evenly between the rollers and back again, the print then being carefully removed and dried.

Roman mosaic
Vide **mosaic**.

Roman sepia
A form of **watercolour** obtained by mixing a yellow pigment with sepia to produce a yellow tone. *Vide* **warm sepia**.

romanesque
Art, architecture and decoration associated with the medieval style of the later Roman empire.

romanticism
Movement in art, literature and music of the 19th and early 20th century, a reaction against **neo-classicism**.

rope
A type of twisted carving, with a form reminiscent of rope.

rose madder
Vide **liquid madder**.

rotunda
A round building, often domed.

rough deals
An interest in the surface effects that can be produced on picture frames toward the end of the 19th century led to the use of oak and then other roughly hewn wood, gilded over with the texture of the wood still visible. Such frames, especially favoured by the Scottish painter Arthur Melville (1855-1904), are known as 'rough deals'.

rouleau
Decoration in the form of a coil or roll of ribbons, also used as trimming.

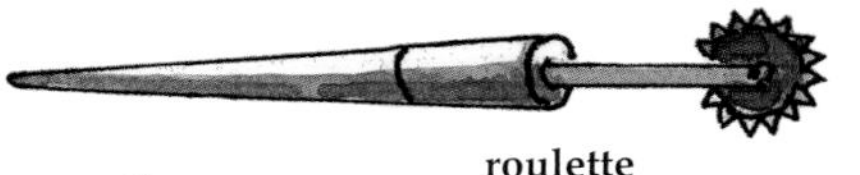

roulette

roulette
Types of tools all with a revolving circular head used for perforating the plate in the preparation of engravings or etchings when **tone presses** are used to simulate coloured washes. The most common forms are the simple roulette, the MATTING WHEEL and the **chalk roller**. A MACE HEAD, a tool with a butt end having irregular points, may also be used.

rubiat
Vide **liquid madder**.

runner
Two meanings: a long, narrow rug, or a dealer who covers small auctions, selling purchases to larger dealers.

running pattern frame
A frame with a running decoration forming a pattern along its sides. Usually carved in **low relief** with scrolling foliage, they were most popular between the mid 1600s and mid 1700s.

rustication
Masonry with a roughened surface or with sunken joints. Also a form of surface decoration used in framing.

S

sable
The colour black.

sacristy
Vide **vestry**.

sail cloth
Vide **canvas**.

Salon
Annual exhibitions held under the auspices of the Royal Academy of Painting and Sculpture in Paris from 1667. After 1881, when it changed hands, its influence and reputation diminished.

saltire
The St Andrew's cross. In heraldry, an 'X'-shaped **Ordinary**.

Salvador Rosa frame
Vide **Carlo Maratta**.

samovar
A large Russian urn, generally of copper, for making tea.

sampler
A panel of **embroidery** used as an exercise by beginners learning the art of needlework. The earliest English examples were made in the first half of the 17th century. Later examples, often signed and dated, were generally the work of children.

sand
Vide **chalcedony**.

sanding
Refers to the **frieze** of a frame which has had sand applied. An 18th century process which was preceded by the application of **gesso** and **gilt**.

sang-de-boeuf
A deep red colour first associated with early Chinese **porcelain**; much copied by later European porcelain manufacturers.

sans-serif
A printing term indicating the absence of **serifs**.

Sansovino
Late 16th and early 17th century type of frame in the **Mannerist** style, most common in Venice, characterised by interlaced **volutes** and scrolls, often **rusticated**. Named after the architect and sculptor Jacopo Tatti Sansovino (1486-1570).

Sansovino

sarcophagus
A stone coffin, often carrying inscriptions and fine commemorative sculptures.

sardonyx
Vide **chalcedony**.

satin
A fabric made of real or simulated silk, occasionally used for making fine prints of the 17th and 18th centuries.

satyr
Lusty, drunken woodland mythological creatures represented in Greek art by the ears and tail of a horse and by the Romans with the ears, horns and tail of a goat.

S

Saxon style
Vide **Byzantine**.

scagliola
An Italian method of imitating stone to simulate highly figured marble, made from a mixture of pure plaster and glue, with added colour.

scalpel
A small flat-bladed knife used by painters for applying oil paint thickly. Shaped to be held like a pen.

scape
Vide **apophyge**.

scauper
An engraver's tool with a semi-circular face for cleaning between the engraved lines.

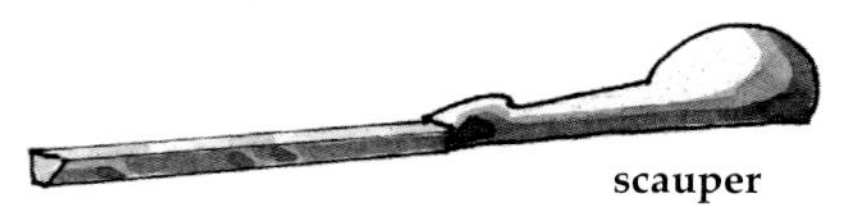

scauper

schiavona
A kind of basket-hilted broadsword, of which the Scottish claymore is an example, popular in Renaissance Italy. Also the title of a famous Titian portrait of a lady, *La Schiavone*.

schlag leaf
Vide **dutch metal**.

schmalz
From the German for 'cooking fat'. In art it refers to any graphic or musical composition that is overly florid or sweetly sentimental.

schmelze
From the German for 'enamel'. Schmelze is a specially coloured glass used in decoration. It can be deep red coloured stained glass, or filigree glass of all kinds, and for glass which changes colour in reflection although deep red in transmitted

light. SCHMELZE AVENTURIN is an opaque brown glass upon which **aventurin** is thinly layered, sometimes known as **goldstone**.

sciagraphy
The treatment of shading in a drawing. In architecture a SCIAGRAPH is the geometrical representation of a vertical section of a construction, illustrating its interior structure. A further use is in astronomy denoting the use of shadows to indicate time. Not to be confused with SCIAMACHY (fighting shadows, shadow boxing).

scoop
The front **hollow** of a frame.

scooper
A gouging tool used in engraving to produce fine lines on the plate. The head may be one of several slightly differing shapes depending on the shape and fineness of the lines required. Also known as a SCORPER.

scotia
A concave **moulding**, often at the base of a **column**. In framing it may be differentiated into an inner and outer scotia depending on its position in the frame.

scraper
Engraver's tool used for removing those parts of the **burr** produced by the **rocker** where highlights should appear. The implement usually has two cutting edges.

scraper board
A chalk surfaced black printed board upon which lines are cut by means of a sharp needle or nib, lightly used as in writing.

scratched out
A technique used in watercolour drawing where the paint is scratched out in places to reveal the white under-surface.

screen printing
Vide **silk screen printing**.

scrimshaw
Sailors' carved or engraved designs on bone or **ivory**. Can also refer to the decorated article itself.

scroll
A curling **volute** reminiscent of a partially unfurled paper scroll.

scudella
An ornamental bowl.

sculp(tit)
Indicates the sculptor, usually preceding the name. *Vide* **caelevit**, **incidit**.

sculpture
The art of making three-dimensional forms. Materials used can be casting metal, stone, clay, or wood, modelled usually by means of a chiselling tool. *Vide* **maquette**. Also refers to the finished product, i.e. a sculpture. A SCULPTOR is one who makes sculptures.

scumble
To soften a drawing or painting. In treating oils a semi-transparent neutral colour is lightly rubbed over that part of the work needing to be subdued, with a soft dry brush. Drawings are treated by lightly rubbing the blunt point of a chalk over the chosen area.

secondary colours
Produced when any two of the **primary colours** are combined in equal measure. Blue and yellow produce green; blue and red produce violet; yellow and red give orange. Excess of a primary colour produces a shade of grey.

Second Empire
Period in French history under Napoleon III 1852-1870.

sedilia
Seats on the south side of the **chancel** in Christian churches for the use of clergy.

sema(i)nier
A tall narrow chest, typically containing seven drawers, popular in continental Europe.

S

Senneh knot
One of the two main kinds of knots used in the weaving of Oriental carpets and rugs. Also known as the **Persian knot**, it is the most common type of knot in Central Asia and the Far East. Made by passing the thread under one warp thread and then round over the next, thus showing a PILE-END between every warp thread. *Vide* **Ghiordes knot**.

sepia
A black secretion or ink produced by the cuttlefish; in art it is the pigment prepared from this liquid. The *sepia officinalis*, common in the Mediterranean, is especially valued for the profusion of colour it provides. The secretion is insoluble in water but extremely diffusable through it. It is washed thoroughly in water before being allowed to gradually subside after which the water is drained away, leaving a black sediment. When prepared with caustic dye it is transformed in to a beautiful brown colour commonly used in drawings and printed illustrations. *Vide* **Roman sepia**, **warm sepia**.

sepic
An archaic term meaning of or pertaining to sepia or a drawing done in sepia.

seraph(im)
An angel of the second **order**, usually depicted with wings and a flaming heart. Symbolic of love, purity and divine affection. Seraphim is the plural. *Vide* **order**.

Senneh knot

serif
A printing term denoting a small projection attached to a letter. Thus, for example, T with serif becomes T. *See also* **sans-serif**.

serigraph
Vide **silk screen print**.

serpentine
Shaped like a serpent. Also a soft rock used for decoration on account of its highly polished appearance.

Sèvres
Fine French porcelain from the mid 18th century, patronised by Louis XV and Madame de Pompadour. Characterised by detailed decoration on a richly coloured ground.

sfumato
The technique of merging colours and tones in the most gradual way. *Vide* **penumbra**.

sgrafitto
A decoration made by scratching through wet plaster or through a **slip** in **ceramics**, illuminating an under-surface of a different colour. In framing, it is generally used to reveal **gold** underneath.

shade
When used as a verb, it means to darken a watercolour or oil painting by introducing black with a colour. The opposite of **tint**.

shadow box
A framing structure in which a painting, framed or unframed, is placed within a shallow box of polished hardwood **mouldings**, usually lined with velvet.

shagreen
An untanned or slightly tanned leather originally obtained from the hides of the wild asses of Iran and Turkey. The term now refers to shark skin and to a rougher form, **galuchet**, taken from dogfish and the spiny skinned ray (*Raja fallonica*). Original shagreen has natural surface granulation whereas modern forms are hard, with a horny texture.

shakudo
An attractive metal **alloy** developed in Japan for making ornamental metalwork. An alloy of copper and up to 10% gold which, after boiling in a solution of copper sulphate, **alum** and **verdigris**, has a bluish black **patina**.

shard
A broken fragment of glass or pottery. A **potsherd**.

Sheffield Plate
Articles made of copper coated by fusion with silver. The process, accidentally discovered in 1742 by Thomas Bolsover (1705-1788), lapsed with the introduction of SILVER-PLATING by electro-deposition in the mid 19th century.

shell cameo
Vide **cameo**.

shellac
A **seed lac** resin used in the making of **varnish**.

S

sheveret
Writing case on legs with small drawers and a lifting handle.

shibayama
Japanese method of encrustation on lacquer and ivory.

shingle
A rectangular wooden tile used for roofing.

shippo
Japanese term referring to the number 7 and to the value or richness of the materials used in the making of an object, whether man-made (e.g. **cloisonné**) or natural (e.g. a **precious stone**).

sight
In picture framing, sight refers to that part of the frame which is exposed to view at the edges.

sight edge
The inner edge of a frame nearest the picture.

significant form
Vide **form**.

S

silhouette
Named after the French writer Étienne de Silhouette (1709-1767). An early form of portraiture showing only the outline, usually in solid black on a white background or cut out of paper. Popular in early Mediterranean art but fell out of fashion with the advent of photography. Recently, the method has enjoyed a revival although with only limited popularity.

silica
Silicon dioxide. A hard colourless or white refractory solid used in the production of **porcelain**. It is hard and in an oxyhydrogen flame fuses to produce an amorphous glass. In the natural world it is very common, known as **quartz**.

silk screen print
A print made by applying colour through a silk or nylon screen, the weave being extremely fine, allowing the paint to reach areas not blanked by stencils. Common in the Orient but in the west mainly in the 20th century. Also called a **serigraph**.

silvering
Term used in framing referring to the use of silver leaf. Requires a finished **lacquer** to prevent tarnishing.

silver point
A device used by early **masters** when sketching in the open air or when travelling, before the advent of pencils. A piece of silver wire held in wood was used to draw on paper coated with an opaque white to which a slight tint of colour was added.

simultaneity
The visual effect when different colours of the spectrum are isolated and applied beside each other. Robert Delaunay (1885 -1941) explored this phenomenon, first illustrated by the French chemist Michel Eugène Chevreul (1786-1889), which came to influence late **Expressionism**.

sinister
In heraldry, the left-hand side; when viewed by an observer it would be on the right. *Vide* **dexter**.

Situationism
The ideology of a small group of left-wing anarchic agitators formed in 1957. It later split into separate groups the most important of which was the SITUATIONIST BAUHAUS. Art and politics were regarded as inseparable while artistic creation stemmed from the union of absolute freedom and rebellious thinking. A key founding figure was the Danish artist Asger Oluf Jurgensen (1914-1973).

size
Gelatinous solution, made from animal skin or parchment clippings, used in framing to make **gypsum** and to preserve unburnished **water gilding**. Also used as an adhesive for **gold leaf** and for other purposes with paper and textiles.

sleeper
An item at auction which fetches or is expected to fetch significantly less than its true market worth. *Vide* **ringer**.

slip
An inserted flat or bevelled strip, generally of thin wood or paper, fitted in the **rebate** of a frame. Can also refer to a creamy liquid used to decorate **pottery**.

soapstone
A kind of **stearite**.
Also known as **potstone**.

soapstone porcelain
Soft paste porcelain using finely ground **stearite** instead of **china clay**. This made it heavier, stronger and with a harder texture than other soft pastes. English manufacturers specialising in this process were Bristol 1748-1752, Caughley 1775-1779, Liverpool until 1772, and Worcester 1751-1824.

Social Realism
Art whose primary purpose is to illustrate perceived social injustice or decay.
Vide **Ashcan school**.

socle
A small **pedestal** in a frame often in the form of a bracket. Derived from the architectural term for a plain low block supporting a **column**.

sofa table
Vide **Pembroke** table.

soffit
The underside of an architectural feature.

soft ground etching
A procedure dating from the mid 18th century whereby the plate has a softer wax ground containing more animal fat than is the case in an ordinary etching. Commonly used by Thomas Gainsborough (1727-1788) and other East Anglian artists of the period. The process involves a sheet of thin paper laid over the ground upon a pencil drawing. When the paper is removed, some of the wax adheres to where the pencil has pressed. The plate is then

immersed in a container of **mordants** and bitten (as for an ordinary etching).

solander
A box for holding prints and manuscripts in the form of a book. Named after the Swedish botanist Daniel Charles Solander (1736-1782).

solomonic column
A twisted **column**.

spandrel
In architecture, the almost triangular space between one side of the outer curve of an **arch** or wall, and the ceiling or framework. In framing it describes a shaped additional inner structure filling the space between a rectangular frame and an oval or circular picture.

S

spelter
A crude form of smelted zinc, an inferior metal used for making sculptures.

sperone
Vide **ante**.

sphinx
An Egyptian mythological monster of which there were three different forms: the ANDRO SPHINX, having the head of a male deity; CRIO SPHINX, with the head of a ram and the body of a lion; and the HIERACO SPHINX, with the head of a hawk and the body of a lion. Later these forms came to be used as ornamentations by other peoples.

Spin Art
A late 20th and early 21st century method of creating so-called art by means of a spinning platform which distributes paint arbitrarily by centrifugal force on to a canvas or other surface. Although generally introduced to interest children, some avant garde artists have experimented with the technique principally among them Damien Hirst (b. 1965) and Alfons Schilling (b. 1934).

spire
A tapering construction on a building, especially a church tower. Usually built on a series of recessed arches built across the angles of a tower, called SQUINCHES.

splay
A spread in a sloping area of a building as when the opening in a wall for a door widens from the position of the door toward the face of the wall. As a verb, to splay is to spread widely.

spline
As a framing term a spline is a piece of wood inserted in to a groove parallel and perpendicular to a **mitred joint**.

spring
Vide **apophyge**.

squinches
Vide **spire**.

s-scroll
A scroll in the shape of an 'S', sometimes with a foliage overlay, used to ornament the sides of **rococo frames**.

Staffordshire
The centre of English ceramics in the 19th century, particularly associated with pottery figures made between 1840 and 1910.

stained glass
Designs using coloured glass, most commonly in church windows. Techniques of colouring and placement have been known since the 11th century and, continuing strongly until the end of the 15th century, stained glass design has enjoyed a strong revival in the last hundred years.

standard
In heraldry, it is a long narrow armorial forked flag. Not to be confused with BANNER which is a larger armorial flag of normal shape.

state
In art, state has two separate meanings. The first is synonymous with condition. The second describes a print in which changes have been made in its various issues, copies from the original being referred to by their different states.

stearite
Soapstone. An impure form of magnesium silicate used in the manufacture of soft paste **porcelain**.

steel-facing
The use of steel applied to a plate by electrolysis to render the copper more durable. A method often used when a large number of **impressions** are required.

steel plate
Any engraving in which steel plates are used instead of copper plates. A hard steel of special value for engraving was developed by Thomas Lupton (1791-1873) in 1820.

steeple
A lofty construction in a building containing the bells.

stele
An upright pillar, often embellished with a formalised sculpture, frequently used by the Greeks as a gravestone.

stencil
A thin plate or sheet of card or metal for cutting letters or a pattern on a surface beneath, before ink or paint is applied. In print making the plate is generally metal.

stereobate
The foundation or solid platform upon which a building is erected. When designed in two steps the upper is known as the **stylobate**.

stereotype
In print making a stereotype is a metal cast used instead of wood engraving for **relief** printing and **embossing**.

stick lac
Vide **lac**.

still life

A painting or drawing of flowers, dead game, or other inanimate objects.

stippling

A technique used especially by engravers and miniaturists using dots and flecks, usually in conjunction with lines; *vide* **hatching**. First recorded in Italy in the 15th century. To stipple is to gradually change colour in a design and this is seen, for example, in stipple engraving when the composition has a dotted outline with the darker areas also marked with dots before being laid in larger and deeper shades. The plate is then bitten-in, the ground removed and the lighter tints laid-in with a STIPPLING TOOL.

stoa

A roofed **portico** sometimes of two storeys.

stone cameo

Vide **cameo**.

stoneware

A form of **pottery** made from a large proportion of **silica**, partly vitrified in the kiln, producing a waterproof, sturdier version of **earthenware**.

stopping out

The use of protective varnish applied to a plate in an etching to avoid damage from further action by the acid.

strapwork

A band of carved ornament reminiscent of plaited straps, often formalized. *Vide* **guilloche**.

straw mosaic

Mosaic made from fine straw in different shades applied with an adhesive to a cardboard foundation.

stretcher

A wooden frame over which a canvas is stretched to hold a painting.

stripwork

Vide **lesene**.

stucco

Plaster used for decoration in interiors and for moulding figures. A rougher version is employed for external use.

stump work

Raised embroidered work, popular in the mid 17th century. The craftsmanship was usually excellent although the pictorial designs were quite primitive. Primarily used as covers for domestic boxes and cushions but also sometimes as pictures. Good examples remain popular with collectors.

style

Distinctive manner of presentation. It may be that of an individual, a group or artistic movement, a place, a period, a genre, a form of treatment.

stylobate

Vide **stereobate**.

sulphur tint

In order to obtain a textile **grain** on an **aquatint** the grain on the plate can be corroded by the use of powdered sulphur evenly spread across a plate that has been moistened with oil. *Vide* **acid tint**.

Sunderland
A frame in the **auricular style** common in the second half of the 17th century. Named after Robert Spencer, 2nd Earl of Sunderland (1640-1702).

Sunderland

sunstone
Vide **aventurin**.

Superrealism
Vide **photorealism**.

Suprematism
Russian version of **abstract art** introduced by Kasimir Malevich (1878-1935) in 1913. A totally non-figurative art form with no reference to the natural world.

surface painting
Vide **relief**.

Surrealism
A movement in **modern art** which, whilst appreciating the importance of content, concentrated most on the imaginative and fantastical. Originating in 1924, it was a natural developments from **Dadaism**. Influenced by Freud, it represented artistic freedom from all conventional restraints. Sometimes with the introduction of visual punning humour (René Magritte, 1898-1967), sometimes by reaching the limits of the sensational (Salvador Dali, 1904-1989), sometimes by the grotesque elongation of the human figure (the Swiss sculptor Alberto Giacometti, 1901-1966). The German painter Max Ernst (1881-1976) added to the genre by inventing **frottage**.

swag
An ornamental **festoon** of flowers on a picture frame, fastened at each end and hanging down in the middle.

swag

sweep
The curving outer edge of a **rococo frame**.

swept
Any frame having sweeping curves, usually of a **rococo** type.

symbol
A design representing something without words, e.g. **Chinese emblems**.

Synchronism
An art movement, originating in the United States, based upon the supposition that colour in a work of art and sound in a musical composition are phenomena which each can reflect.

T

tabernacle

Tabernacle

A **Kent frame** characterised by **architectonic** structural and decorative surrounds. The name comes from the ornamental niche above an altar, influencing a 15th century form of this kind of frame.

tableau

A picturesque arrangement of people or objects. TABLEAU CURTAINS are an arrangement of curtains drawn together as in a theatre.

tabouret

A stool with an embroidered or linen top, designed for women. Made originally for ladies of high rank permitted to be seated when in the presence of the king. Similar to a **buffet stool**.

tachisme

Mid 20th century French method of abstract colour painting using a random distribution of paint thought to induce subconscious feelings.

taenia

An architectural term describing a **fillet** between a **Doric architrave** and **frieze**. Derived from the Greek word for ribbon.

taenia

taille douce

Vide **line engraving**.

Taisho

The period in Japan, immediately following the **Meiji**, named after the Emperor Taisho who reigned 1912-1926.

Talbotype
Vide **calotype**.

talisman
Vide **amulet**.

tansu
Vide **kodansu**.

tantalus
A decanter with a locking device.

tapestry
A fabric of coloured threads in various materials producing a pattern or artistic composition, generally for use as wall coverings. The best known and highest quality examples are Aubusson, at its height during the reign of Louis XIV, Gobelin of Paris and its followers at Neuilly, and Russian tapestry.

Tassie
A cameo replica of an **intaglio** or glass paste impression, called after James Tassie (1735-1799) who specialised in making these gems after settling in London in 1766.

taste
There are several distinct but closely related meanings: (1) artistic discrimination. This develops with experience, whether it be in one's choice of art, furniture or wine. With no real experience there can be no real taste. (2) A style or manner of a national or local kind e.g. the French taste. (3) To experience meaningful exposure to artistic form.

tau
A T-shaped cross.

tazza
A bowl or shallow vase shaped like a saucer, often with handles and a foot.

teapoy
A small table designed for individual tea drinking. When teapots became larger in the late 18th century, the delicate size grew to become an ornamental pedestal table large enough to hold equipment for a tea party of four.

tempera
Distemper. A medium used in painting which uses water and egg yolk as a binder. In general use before the advent of oils in the 15th century. In Italy, tempera, *fresco a seco*, is distinguished from *fresco buono* which is painted on newly laid **stucco**.

temperature
Vide **colour**.

tenon
Vide **mortice**.

terminus
A sculpture or bronze when only the upper part of the body is depicted, terminating in a plain rectangular block.

terra cotta
A type of unglazed brownish red **earthenware** used primarily for ceramic modelling and ornamental building

material. The colour varies according to the ingredients. It may have an enamelled or coloured surface.

tertiary colours
Produced by a mixture of two **secondaries**. Tertiaries are citrine, olive and russet. When a **primary colour** predominates, citrine is yellowish grey, olive is bluish grey and russet is reddish grey. When a secondary is dominant the hues become greenish grey, violet grey or rouge grey.

tessera
A small piece of hard material, generally square, used in combination with others to make **mosaics**. Tesserae differ from tiles in having a smaller surface and being proportionately thicker. The diminutive term is TESSELLA.

textile ground
A method of creating an **etching** with a textile effect, produced by a sheet of material laid on to a waxed ground and rolled through a press. A development of **soft ground etching**.

throw(n)
To shape pottery on the potter's wheel, known also as a THROWING ENGINE. Hence THROWN WARE are pottery objects thrown on the potter's wheel, encompassing all pottery except only the coarsest. A THROWING TABLE is a contrivance which turns the wheel mechanically. THROWING CLAY is clay sufficiently plastic to be used in the making of pottery. A THROWING HOUSE, or THROWING MILL, is the place wherein the potter's wheel is housed.

thurible
Vide **censer**.

tier étagère
A **dumb waiter**, generally with two tiers and often on wheels.

Tiffany

Tiffany
American glass of the art nouveau period, developed by Charles Tiffany (1812-1902).

tint
As a verb, to add white to a colour to heighten the brightness, often employed in engraving by cutting parallel lines on a woodblock to produce a light shading.

tint tool
An engraver's form of **scraper** but with a triangular section used for cutting very fine lines.

tole-peinte
A painted tinware object.

toleware
Any varnished (japanned) **pewter** or tinplate.

tonal value
Vide **colour**.

tondo
A frame with circular **sight** and back edges. In ceramics it is a plate or dish with a flat, wide rim, often seen in Italian **majolica**.

tone processes
Any method of engraving or etching which has the intention of achieving layers of tone similar to a coloured wash.

tongue
Any ornament shaped like a tongue, e.g. **egg-and-tongue**.

top edge
The most prominent **moulding** of a frame.

torc
A twisted metal necklace, most common among the Gauls and ancient Britons, often made of gold. Also spelt TORQUE.

torchère
A tall stand with a table top designed to support a lamp. Generally an elegant item of furniture, also known as a **gueridon**.

tortoiseshell
The outer shell or one of the scales of certain sea turtles, especially the hawksbill turtle. Widely used in the manufacture of many domestic objects but also in ornamental work especially snuff boxes, and occasionally for framing. Artificial imitations are cheaper and increasingly common although inferior.

torus
A large convex **moulding**, generally semi-circular in section. Usually seen as the lowest part of the base of a **column**. Similar to an **ovolo**.

tourelle
A miniature turret projecting from the main wall above the ground.

tracery
Specifically, in architecture, ornamental openwork built into a window as in early churches; generally, a decorative line unrelated to anything in nature.

tracery

transept
A throughway along the arm of a conventionally shaped church at right angles to the nave.

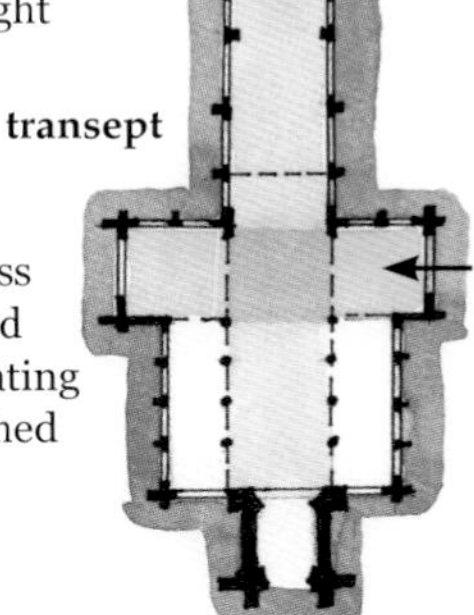
transept

transfer printing
In ceramics a process of applying engraved decorations, originating in 1753. Distinguished from hand painted decoration.

treen
Small wooden domestic objects, most often kitchen and tableware. From the Anglo-Saxon *triwen* meaning wooden. *Vide* **trencher**.

trellis
An interwoven or interlaced supporting structure usually made of metal or wood. Also used as a verb, and a type of armour.

trencher
A wooden plate; also a slice of bread upon which to place food; also whatever the trencher may contain. There are many hyphenated related terms of obvious

meaning e.g. TRENCHERMAN (one who serves at table).

triforium
The area in a church above the **transept**, **choir** and **nave**.

triglyphs
In architecture, a series of tablets with three vertical grooves, alternating with **metopes**, in a **Doric frieze**. By extension, a similar arrangement of shapes in a picture frame. The grooves are known as **glyphs**.

triptych
A group of three paintings or a **relief** carving on three panels, usually hinged vertically together, often as altar-pieces. The central panel may be double the width of the side panels.

trompe-l'oeil
A **still life** painting composed so as to deceive the eye in to believing it to be three dimensional.

trophy
On frames it describes an applied trophy or coat of arms, usually carved with a gilt finish projecting from the main structure and symbolic of the sitter or subject of the picture.

truncated
The top of an object cut off parallel to the base.

Turkish carpets
Vide **Oriental carpets**.

turnery
Part of the craft of furniture making, using a lathe to mould (turn) wood into different shapes. The changing methods and styles of turning, especially of furniture legs, is a useful indicator of period.

Tuscan
The least ornamental of the five classical orders of architecture. Developed by the Romans, with no **fluting** to the **columns**. Similar to the Roman **Doric**.

tyg
A flat bottomed drinking vessel, often with three or four handles, designed to be passed round the company on ceremonial occasions. Also spelled TIG.

tympan
An appliance in a printing press, inserted between the plates and the sheet to be printed, used to soften or equalise the pressure.

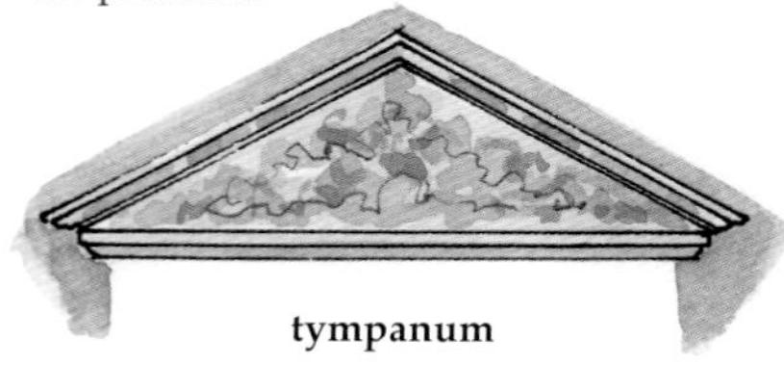

tympanum

tympanum
A vertical triangular space forming the centre of a **pediment**. In framing it refers to the surface between the upper and lower **cornices** of a pediment.

type
A right-angled prism shaped piece of metal or wood.

typography
The art of printing.

U

ultramarine
A blue **pigment** obtained by grinding a lazulite stone, calcinating, and then grinding again. An expensive but highly regarded colour.

underglaze (painting)
Paint on porcelain before applying a **glaze**. The underglaze is the surface prepared to receive the glaze.

unicorn
A mythical horse like creature with a single long and twisted horn, a goat's beard, and cloven hooves. Symbol of beauty and power. Regarded as a dangerous animal hence the chain which appears in early heraldry and, for example, in the Arms of King James V of Scotland.

unicorn

Universal Flowering
Vide **Futurism**.

V

valuation

Valuation for probate and insurance should be given in writing and should refer to the replacement value, according to the current market worth of a given work by the same artist, of similar size and composition. Valuations or offers to a potential vendor should refer to the wholesale value.

value

In artistic terms it has a variety of different and not necessarily related denotations. It can refer to the specific value of an object in financial terms or to its innate quality, as attributed by art experts i.e. its 'true' worth. Value can also refer to the subjective pleasure derived from ownership, regardless of objective value. An object may have 'great' value to its owner, e.g. a gift from a loved one, irrespective of commercial worth.

varnish

A liquid applied to a painting to help in its preservation and to give a transparent, slightly glossy finish. Varnishes are resinous solutions which vary according to the intensity of the finish they provide.

veduta

A landscape painting sufficiently accurate to locate it geographically.

veneer

A thin slice of wood or stone laid on similar material made to look like a solid mass. Often used in **marquetry** and other kinds of decorative panelling.

Venetian frame

A type of ornately carved picture frame generally with bold, open scrolling. Similar to the **Florentine type**. *Vide* **'Pitti Palace'** frames.

Venetian mosaic

Vide **mosaic**.

verde antique

An ornamental stone highly valued by the Romans. A form of serpentine quarried in Europe, Egypt and eastern United States. Unsuitable for outdoor use.

vernacular

In architecture it refers to a simple building characteristic of a region.

verre églomisé
The glass border of a mirror ornamented on the underside by a design backed by a gilt or silver leaf usually against a background of red or black. Popular in the early 18th century.

vestry
A room attached to a church for storage and other purposes by the clergy. Also called a **sacristy**.

vignette
A decoration or decorative design, especially on the title page of a book or around the text on an old map, not enclosed within a clear border. Originally applied to a capital letter in an ancient manuscript ornamented with flourishes reminiscent of young vine leaves.

virtu
Knowledge about the **fine arts**. More commonly used to include unusual small, decorative objects (**curios**) having some commercial value due to either their antiquity, craftsmanship, or unusual character. Also spelt VERTU.

vitrine
A show case for the display of small delicate articles such as ceramics or glass. Not to be confused with **citrine**.

vitruvian scroll
An architectural scroll consisting of a run of convoluted shapes. Frequently employed in **friezes**. Derived from Marcus Vitruvius Pollo, a Roman architect of 1BC.

volute
Generic term for a spiral scroll, characteristic of **Ionic capitals**. Popular in 17th century framing and furniture.

vorticism
An English literary and artistic movement of the early 20th century which arose as a revolt against what was seen as the false sentimentality of the 19th century. Painting and sculpture became harsh and mechanistic. The moving spirit was Wyndham Lewis (1882-1957). Disciples included the sculptors Sir Jacob Epstein (1880-1959) and Henri Gaudier-Brzeska (1891-1915), also the painters William Roberts (1895-1980) and Edward Wadsworth (1889-1949). The movement enjoyed only a short life but its influence on modern art continues.

voussoir
Architectural term for a stone shaped like a truncated wedge forming part of an **arch**. The middle voussoir is called the **keystone**.

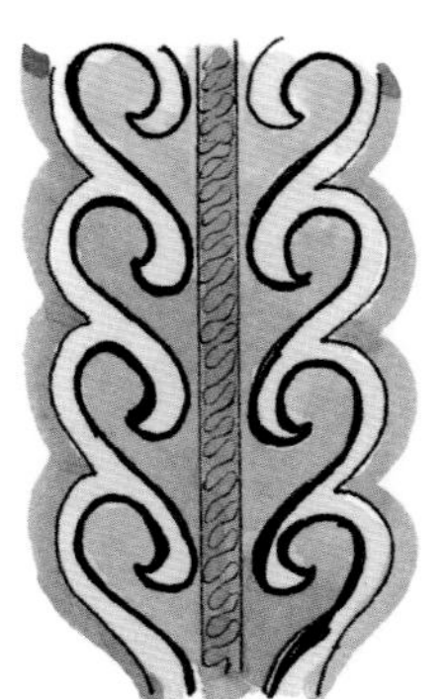

vitruvian scroll

W

warm sepia
A watercolour prepared by mixing red **pigment** with **sepia**. *Vide* **Roman sepia**.

wash
A watery application of colour. This may be used in a watercolour drawing or, more commonly, on a mount. *Vide* **line-and-wash**.

watercolour
Artistic medium where colour is provided by **pigment** mixed with water rather than with oil.

water gilding
The use of a water based gold **size** as adhesive, known as the **bole**, which has to be wetted before gilding.

waterleaf
A small veined leaf used to enrich a **moulding**, often with each waterleaf alternating with a plain tongue.

W

watermark
A distinguishing mark or character in **paper**, more common in laid paper, less in woven paper. Made by the introduction of a wire mesh into the tray in which the pulp settles, the marks becoming visible when held to the light after the paper has dried. A countermark was introduced in the 17th century incorporating more precise details of the manufacturer, appearing opposite the watermark. Watermarks date the paper with the help of reference works such as Heawood's *Watermarks mainly of the 17th and 18th Centuries*, 1950.

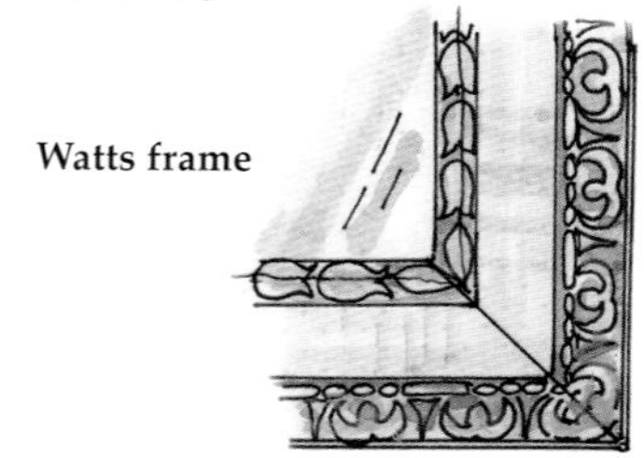
Watts frame

Watts frame
A **box frame**, common in the late 19th century, with the **sight** and **top edges** having leaf ornament in **compo**, the main flat **frieze** often gilded direct on to the oak. Named after the English painter, George Frederick Watts (1817-1904).

weather moulding
Vide **hood mould**.

Wedgwood

A kind of fine English pottery, called after its founder, Josiah Wedgwood (1730-1795). Established a factory named 'Etruria'.

Wemyss

Scottish pottery made in Fife from the early 1880s. Most products are clearly marked with patterns that can be accurately dated.

whatnot

A furniture stand with three or four tiers designed to hold small objects. Often made in pairs, they became popular in the mid 19th century. Also known as an **omnium**. A substantial French form is an ***étagère***, a table with an upper shelf supported on carved or turned columns.

Whistler frame

A popular type of frame, named after the painter, James McNeill Whistler (1834-1903), current from c1870. It can be either a flat frame with inner and outer parallel reeded bands, or as a reeded **cushion frame**, usually with gilt upon oak but sometimes on white-painted pine, and with the parallel reeded lines close together.

white agate

Vide **chalcedony**.

white line engraving

Produced by a wood engraver cutting lines in the wooden block to produce white lines when printed in **relief**.

whiting

Ground chalk used in whitewashing and plate cleaning. An essential ingredient in the making of **gesso**.

wine cooler

Vide **celarette**.

woodcut

A print made from a relief cut on wood prepared along with grain. In good woodcutting black lines should never cross each other. The main advantage is that a woodcut can be printed with less pressure than **line engraving**. Woodcuts declined towards the end of the 16th century but enjoyed a revival in the 19th century.

wood engraving

A print made by a **relief** cut on a block of wood that has been sawn across the grain. The distinction from a **woodcut** is that whereas in the former the knife is applied to the side grain, in a wood engraving the end-grain, with its more even texture, is used.

woodworm

The furniture beetle, *anobium punctatum*, whose larvae creates channels in wood. Also known as **beetle damage**.

Worcester porcelain

English soft paste decorative porcelain dating from 1751. Responsible for introducing transfer printing.

wyvern

A dragon with only two legs and wings resting on a knotted tail. Seen in heraldry and occasionally in the decorative arts. Sometimes spelt WIVERN.

X

xoanon

Primitive wooden Grecian sculptures representing deities. It has come to describe early stone statues showing similar primitive workmanship often with closed eyes and poorly sculpted or absent limbs.

xylography

Painting or engraving on wood or an impression from a woodblock. A secondary meaning is a copy of woodgrain made mechanically for surface decoration.

xylonite

Vide **ivorine**.

Y

yao-pien

The word means literally 'changed in the kiln'. **Porcelain** which, through over-firing or other accident in the kiln, changes in colour from that originally intended. Some of the most valuable pieces of Chinese porcelain have had their colour transformed in this way.

Z

zarf
A metal holder for encompassing a coffee-cup.

ziggurat
Small stepped stonework just above the foot of a column or frontage of a building.

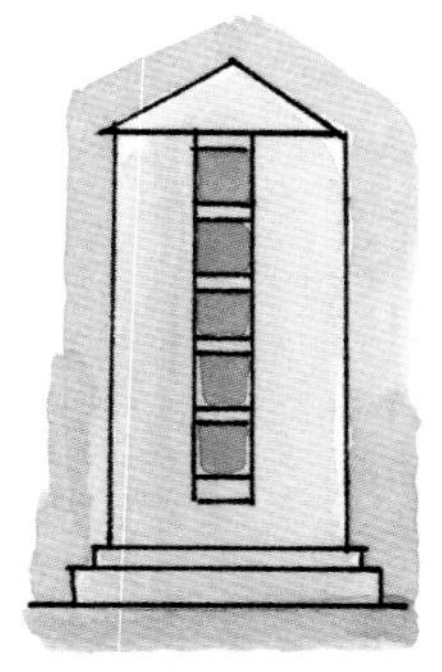

ziggurat

zinc(ograph)
To etch using acid on a zinc plate having on its surface a design for printing. A ZINCOGRAPH refers to the zinc plate and the resultant plate. ZINCOGRAPHY is the art of using the above process.

zitan
Highly valued wood, a member of the rosewood family. Because it is very slow growing and also because of its scarcity and superb texture, it is regarded by the Chinese as the most precious of all timbers. Zitan furniture has great value.

zophoros
A type of **frieze** consisting of an intertwining series of figures in **relief**.

zwischengoldglass
Glass with two layers, having gold decoration in the middle.

zythepsary
An archaic term for a brew-house. Derived from the Greek words for beer and boil.

APPENDICES

Appendix A

British Monarchs
Stuarts, Hanoverians and Windsors

James I	1603-1623
Charles I	1623-1649
[Commonwealth]	1649-1660
Charles II	1660-1685
James II	1685-1688
William III & Mary	1689-1702
Queen Anne	1702-1714
George I	1714-1727
George II	1727-1760
George III	1760-1820
George IV	1820-1830
William IV	1830-1837
Queen Victoria	1837-1901
Edward VII	1901-1910
George V	1910-1936
George VI	1936-1952
Queen Elizabeth II	1952-

Appendix B

Periods of English Architecture (Approximations)

Pre-Norman	Up to 1060
Norman	1060-1190
Early English (Gothic)	1190-1270
Decorated (Gothic)	1270-1370
Perpendicular (Gothic)	1370-1550
English Baroque	1650-1710
Georgian	1710-1820
Victorian	1820-1900
Edwardian	1900-1910

Note: Transitional work occurred throughout and between all later periods.

Appendix C

Periods of English Furniture

Early Oak Period	Early 16th century-1660
Late Tudor	1558-1603
Jacobean	1603 -1649
Commonwealth	1649-1660
Restoration	1660
Early Walnut Period	1660-1690
William & Mary	1689
Later Walnut Period	1690-1720
Queen Anne	1702-1714
Early Georgian Period	1720-1740
Pre-'Director' (Georgian) Period	1740-1754
Thomas Sheraton	1751-1806
Post-'Director' Period	1754-1811
Robert Adam	1728-1792
Thomas Chippendale	1718-1779
George Hepplewhite	c. 1727-1796
The Regency Period	1811-1820
Victorian Period	1820-1900
Edwardian Period	1900-1915

Appendix D

Common Book Sizes

(With variations according to size of paper used)

Elephant Folio	from 25" x 19"		
Folio	from 18" x 11½"		
Quarto			
imperial	15"	x	11"
royal	12½"	x	10"
demi	11¼"	x	8¾"
crown	10"	x	7½"
Octavo			
imperial	11"	x	7½"
royal	10"	x	6¼"
demi	8¾"	x	5½"
crown	7½"	x	5"
Duodecimo	from 5¾" x 4½"		

Appendix E

Japanese Dynasties

Asuka Period		
	Suiko	593 - 628
	Hakuho	674 - 685
Nara Period		
	Tempyo	729 - 784
Early Heian		
	Konin	810 - 823
	Jogan	859 - 876
Middle & Late Heian		
	Fugiwara	898 - 1185
Kamakura Period		1185 - 1333
Muromachi (Ashikaga) Period		
	Nambokucho	1336 - 1393
Momoyama Period		1573 - 1614
Edo (Tokagawa) Period		1615 - 1867
Meiji Restoration		1867 - 1911
Taisho Period		1912 - 1926

Appendix F

Chinese Dynasties

Shang Yin	(?)1766-1122 B.C.
Zhou	(?)1122-249
Zhan Guo	481-221 B.C.
Qin	221-206 B.C.
Han	206B.C.-A.D.220
Liu Chao	220-589
Beiwei	386-535
Liang	502-556
Sui	581-618
Tang	618-906
Wu Dai	907-960
Liao	907-1125
Song	960-1279
Jin	1115-1234
Yuan	1280-1368
Ming	1368-1644
Hong Wu	1368-1398
Jian Wen	1399-1402
Yong Le	1403-1424
Hong Xi	1425
Xuan De	1426-1435
Zheng Tong	1436-1449
Jing Tai	1450-1457
Tian Shun	1457-1464
Cheng Hua	1465-1487
Hong Zhi	1488-1505
Zheng De	1506-1521
Jing Tai	1522-1566
Long Qing	1567-1572
Wan Li	1573-1619
Tai Chang	1620
Tian Qi	1621-1627
Chon Zhen	1628-1643
Qing	1644-1912
Shun Zhi	1644-1661
Kang Xi	1662-1722
Yong Zheng	1723-1735
Qian Long	1736-1795
Jia Qing	1796-1820
Dao Guang	1821-1850
Xian Feng	1851-1861
Tong Zhi	1862-1873
Guang Xu	1874-1908
Xuan Tong	1909-1912
Zhong Hua Min Guo	1912-